Bobbie Rosenfeld

The Olympian Who Could Do Everything

Bobbie Rosenfeld

The Olympian Who
Could Do Everything

ANNE DUBLIN

Second
Story
Press

National Library of Canada Cataloguing in Publication Data

Dublin, Anne
Bobbie Rosenfeld : the Olympian who could do everything / Anne Dublin.

ISBN 1-896764-82-7

1. Rosenfeld, Bobbie, 1904–1969–Juvenile literature. 2. Athletes–Canada–Biography–
Juvenile literature. 3. Sportswriters–Canada–Biography–Juvenile literature. I. Title.

GV697.R68D92 2004   j796'.092   C2004-900833-1

Edited by Sarah Silberstein Swartz
Photo edit by Laura McCurdy
Index by Janice Weaver
Designed by Counterpunch / Peter Ross
Printed and bound in Canada

*Second Story Press gratefully acknowledges the support of the Ontario Arts Council and
the Canada Council for the Arts for our publishing program. We acknowledge the financial
support of the Government of Canada through the Book Publishing Industry Development
Program, and the Government of Ontario through the Ontario Media Development
Corporation's Ontario Book Initiative.*

Published by
Second Story Press
720 Bathurst Street, Suite 301   *20 manol Street, Su*
Toronto, Ontario, Canada
M5S 2R4   *M5V 2M5*
www.secondstorypress.on.ca

For my parents, Gail and Morris Dublin, who have always been my heroes.

"Sports history is replete with the names of forgotten competitors who established outstanding records in their day."

– Bobbie Rosenfeld

Table of Contents

Introduction

Sports are an important part of life for today's young women and men. Girls and boys play hockey, softball, basketball, soccer, track and field, and many other sports. Young people enjoy athletics for fun, for recreation, for the love of the game. If someone is really good at a sport, he or she might even train with a coach. For those who are exceptional, the aim could be to compete in the Olympic Games, held every two years around the world. Whether it's for fun or more serious goals, playing sports is good, healthy exercise for everyone. It teaches you to put your best effort into whatever you do.

But there was a time when opportunities for young people to become athletes were harder to find. Girls, in particular, were discouraged from playing games that were competitive and rough. Well into the 1950s, there was gender discrimination in sports. Girls were considered too fragile and sensitive to play hard and to play well. Doctors warned that competitive sport was bad for women's health. For years, even women sports educators agreed that girls should not "strain" themselves. Up until about fifty years ago, many girls had to disobey their parents in order to play the sports they loved. These girls were often labeled "tomboys" or "roughnecks."

There were many theories behind this stereotype. Some people believed that competition might be too hard on their feelings and that girls would cry if they lost a race. Others believed it was indecent for girls to wear comfortable sports clothes that might show too much skin, like an ankle or an elbow. One "medical" theory was that if girls strained themselves by doing sports, they might be unable to have babies. The final argument was that young women who competed in "unladylike" sports would be less attractive to men and might end up without a husband!

Because of this gender discrimination, girls who wanted to play sports in a serious way experienced many problems. They often received inadequate financial support, inferior equipment and facilities, less convenient practice times, and inexperienced, if any, coaches and teachers. It was hard for young women to compete seriously in any sports event, even on an amateur level. As for professional sports, there was little place for women.

From our perspective in the twenty-first century, we might think these were foolish ideas. But many people up to the 1950s were convinced they were right. How have our attitudes changed?

About one hundred years ago in a small town in Russia, a baby girl was born who would eventually make a difference in how people viewed women in sports. Despite all the obstacles she faced as a woman, she became one of the finest athletes Canada has ever produced. She excelled in many sports: track and field, ice hockey, basketball, softball, and tennis. When she was sent to the Summer Olympics of 1928 as part of the Canadian team, she won two medals. When she could no longer play sports, she coached. When she could no longer coach, she wrote a sports column for an important Canadian newspaper. And always, she was her own person.

When Fanny (Bobbie) was a teenager, many girls and women cut their hair in a new short style called a "bob." Fanny cut her hair, too. From then on, everyone called her "Bobbie."

She was a woman known for her strength and fair play on the sports field, for her wit and honesty off the field. She was one of the first athletes to be honored by Canada's Sports Hall of Fame. As the year 1950 came to a close, the most important sports writers in Canada voted her Canada's "Female Athlete of the Half-Century." A park was named after her, and a historic site devoted to her. Many years after her death, she is still remembered for her great athletic gifts. A fine athlete and advocate for amateur and women's sports, she remains a role model for young women athletes today.

Her parents named her Fanny, but the world came to know her as Bobbie Rosenfeld. This is her story.

I

Beginnings

Above: *Immigrants arriving at Union Station in Toronto, 1910.* ***Facing page:*** *Bobbie, ready for a race.*

Fanny "Bobbie" Rosenfeld was born on December 28, 1904, in the town of Katrinaslov, in the Ukraine, then part of Russia. She was the first daughter of Max and Sarah Rosenfeld, a Jewish couple who would take their two children, Bobbie and Maurice, to a new world in Canada.

In those days, Russia still had a czar, a powerful ruler born into that position, much like a king. But the workers and peasants were gearing up for a major uprising against him and his government. These people wanted a revolution. They were fed up with poverty and hunger, and the huge differences

The exact year when Bobbie Rosenfeld was born is unclear. Some sources say 1903 or 1904. Others suggest 1905. In those days, people did not always keep accurate track of birth dates.

between the lives of the rich and the poor. They reasoned that if revolution had created freedom and liberty for the people in France and in North America, it could also work in Russia.

Many workers and peasants marched and demonstrated against the czar's government. On January 22, 1905 – the day people would later call Bloody Sunday – Russian troops at the Winter Palace in St. Petersburg killed more than one hundred peaceful marchers. It was only a taste of the upheaval and violence that was to come twelve years later.

The name of the town of Katrinaslov was later changed to Dneipropetrovsk. It now has a population of over one million people and is the third-largest city in the Ukraine.

Aside from all these troubles, Russia wasn't a good place to be Jewish. Bandits on horseback started pogroms (riots) in Jewish neighborhoods at the drop of a hat. Because the church and the government supported and even encouraged these bandits, the local police never interfered. Instead they stood by, while mobs beat up Jews and destroyed their property. In 1905, during an especially violent pogrom, more than one thousand Jews were killed in the city of Odessa, also in the Ukraine.

In early 1905, Max and Sarah Rosenfeld decided it was time to leave Russia. Their daughter was only three weeks old when they left for good. The swaying of the ship on that difficult winter crossing made the whole family seasick throughout the voyage.

Immigrants arriving at Union Station in Toronto, 1910. Bobbie's family would have passed through Union Station only a few years earlier.

The food was terrible. The beds were cramped and uncomfortable. It was impossible to take a bath or to wash clothes. Crossing the ocean was an ordeal that no one ever wanted to go through again.

Max and Sarah and their two young children finally arrived safely in Halifax, the port city on the eastern coast of Canada. After a long train ride westward to Toronto and another shorter one, the family ended up in a small Ontario town called Barrie. It is located about 100 kilometers (60 miles) north of Toronto on the western shore of Lake Simcoe. Why did they choose Barrie? Max was the youngest of thirteen children, and his older brother, William, had already settled there. Later, Bobbie said she was happy her parents had moved to Barrie, because it was easier to spell than the place where she had been born!

This was a time when Canada saw the arrival of many immigrants, especially from Eastern Europe – 138,000 in the year 1903 alone. They came from countries all around the world, from England and Ireland, Finland and Iceland, Italy and China, Poland and Russia. They came to find work, to escape persecution, to practice their religion freely, and to make a new home in a land of peace and freedom.

The popular book *The Wonderful Wizard of Oz* by L. Frank Baum had just been published. The paper clip was patented and Crayola crayons were first produced. The Ford Motor Company sold its first automobile, and Orville and Wilbur Wright flew the first powered aircraft at Kitty Hawk, North Carolina.

The third modern Olympic Games was held in St. Louis, Missouri, in 1904. The ice cream cone was invented at the World's Fair, an event that almost overshadowed the Olympics. Many countries did not even bother to send a team to the Olympics, but Canada did. And a Montreal policeman named Etienne Desmarteau won Canada's first Olympic gold medal – in the hammer throw. He was the only non-American to win a medal in track and field during the 1904 Games.

Of course, in 1904, Bobbie was a baby and didn't know that any of these important events were happening around her. But as she grew up, she would learn about some of them, especially about the Olympics.

Bobbie grew up on Collier Street in Barrie, Ontario, pictured here around 1910.

2
Growing Up in Barrie

When Bobbie's parents settled in Barrie, Ontario, Max Rosenfeld went into the junk business. In those days, many Jewish immigrants from Eastern Europe started out as peddlers. Once they became more familiar with life in Canada, they often set up a store in a small town. There were very few jobs available to them, yet they had to make enough money to support their families. Life was not easy for the new immigrants.

The Rosenfeld family lived over their store at 33 Collier Street, opposite the Trinity Anglican Church. A parking lot now sits on the spot where the store used to stand. Max set up shop with one door on the street side and another in the back lane. The sign at the front read, "Antiques sold here." The one at the back read, "Junk bought here." Someone might bring an old battered container into the store. Max would hammer out all the dents, shine it up, and sell it as a beautiful vase. Whatever he couldn't sell, he broke into smaller pieces and sold to scrap metal dealers. With a mismatched set of dishes, Max would wait until similar dishes came in, combine the good pieces, and sell it as a complete set of delicate china. It took patience and skill, but Max knew how to turn junk into antiques. He used a horse and wagon to make his pick-ups and deliveries.

When Max set up his shop in Barrie, he didn't realize that he wouldn't be allowed to keep his store open on Sundays. After 1907, it was against the law to operate a business on the Christian Sabbath. So, he had a hard choice to make: to keep his store running on Saturday, the Jewish Sabbath, or to lose two days' business. He needed to support his family, so the store remained open on Saturdays. Since the family wasn't especially religious, it seemed the sensible thing to do.

Small-town Barrie had a population of about 7,000. Almost everyone in the area was Catholic or Protestant and almost everyone was white. One could count the number of Black, You Chinese, or Jewish families living in the town on the fingers of one hand. Though they stood out as different, these minorities were generally tolerated.

Except for customers, the Rosenfelds kept mostly to themselves. It must have been a lonely life for them, with few

Main Street in Barrie, Ontario, around 1907.

Growing Up in Barrie

other Jewish families with whom to celebrate holidays or special events. There were too few Jews to set up a synagogue or community center in Barrie. Their only link with Jewish culture came from the Yiddish newspapers that were mailed from Toronto or New York. They longed for a Jewish community with other newcomers who spoke familiar languages – Yiddish and Russian. Max and Sarah had to learn English through trial and error with their customers. In those days, there were no English classes for immigrants – children or adults.

If business was slow, or if Max was ill, the family had to struggle on. People who were poor or sick depended on charity, usually given out by Christian churches or upper-class women's aid societies. Sarah didn't have the modern conveniences we have today. She used oil lamps for light and an icebox, an early form of the refrigerator before electricity, to keep food fresh. She cooked on a wood-burning stove. The toilet was an outhouse in the backyard.

Max and Sarah Rosenfeld's family grew. The couple had three more girls: Gertie, Mary, and Ethel. The children had an active life growing up in small-town Canada – swimming in the lake during the summers and skating during the winters. Bobbie loved to play all kinds of sports on corner lots, in town parks, and on outdoor rinks – jumping, running, softball, basketball, and ice hockey. She played mostly with her older brother, Maurice, and his friends. Maurice was especially good at swimming and ice hockey. Bobbie didn't swim well, but could she ever skate! She handled the puck and body-checked with the best of the boys. All that playing against her brother's friends made Bobbie a tough competitor.

Bobbie ran her first race because she was hungry. One hot summer day, she went to a picnic with her family to Minesing, a town west of Barrie. Somehow, she and her sister Gertie got separated from the family. And, what was worse, separated from the picnic lunch! They weren't as much worried as they were hungry. When Bobbie heard there was a 50-yard race for girls and the prize was lunch, she and Gertie entered the race. Bobbie dashed across the finish line, easily ahead of all the other girls. She looked back, grabbed Gertie's arm and hauled her across the line, too. By then, they were even hungrier and quickly ate up their prize – hot dogs, ice cream, and soda pop. Bobbie was nine years old at the time and Gertie was seven.

As Bobbie was growing up, it was an exciting time for sports, a time for firsts. The first international soccer tournament was played in 1908. The first women's automobile race occurred in 1909. In the first decade of the twentieth century, Tom Longboat, from the Six Nations Reserve near Brantford, Ontario, became a famous long-distance runner. At the Boston Marathon in 1907, Longboat crossed the finish line in 2 hours, 24 minutes, 25 seconds, setting a new record for the 25-mile course. Competition became fiercer when the stopwatch was able to measure time with increasing accuracy. The National Hockey League was formed in 1917, and Canadian hockey hasn't looked back since.

During World War I (1914 to 1918), then called the "Great War," many men went off to fight in Europe. Some never came back. While the men were gone, women went to work in factories, stores and other businesses. Suddenly, there were more single women who had time to fill after work and many of them took up sports. Three of the most popular activities were ice hockey, basketball, and softball. Women played to amuse

- The second decade of the twentieth century saw two tragic disasters: In 1912, the *Titanic* hit an iceberg and sank in the North Atlantic Ocean off the coast of Newfoundland. At least 1,500 passengers and crew lost their lives. Seven hundred people, mostly women and children, were rescued.

- A new invention called the "wireless" (or radio) saved many people by sending a distress signal to the rescue ship, the *Carpathia*. The radio also told people around the world the names of the survivors.

- Later in the decade, on December 6, 1917, two ships collided in Halifax harbor. One of them, the *Mont-Blanc*, was loaded with ammunition headed for the Great War in Europe. When the ship exploded, people over 300 kilometers (180 miles) from the blast felt the shock waves. As far as seventy-five kilometers (fifty miles) away, windows shattered. Houses, factories, schools, and churches were knocked down. Six square kilometers (two square miles) of Halifax were flattened. More than two thousand people were killed and nine thousand were wounded.

Three women hockey players at Varsity Arena, Toronto, in 1910.

Growing Up in Barrie

themselves and to meet new friends. Sometimes they played to raise money for the war effort. Always they played to keep their minds off the fact that fathers or brothers or husbands were fighting, and maybe dying, in the faraway war.

Of course, some women had been playing sports since the late nineteenth century. Golf, tennis, archery, sailing, cycling, curling, badminton, and even croquet were considered appropriate sports for women. They did not participate in the "manly" sports – team games such as cricket, soccer, rugby, lacrosse, football, and baseball. When they played, they wore long skirts and blouses buttoned to the neck and wrists, so that they would keep their modest, ladylike appearance. It was mostly upper-class women who participated in sports in those years. They were university students or members of elite country clubs. When working-class women started to participate in sports in the second decade of the twentieth century, big changes came about.

From *Blackwood's Magazine*, 1890: "She can swim, she can dance, she can ride: all these she can do admirably and with ease herself. But to run, nature most surely did not construct her. She can do it after a fashion, just as the domestic hen will on occasion make shift to fly; but the movement is constrained and awkward – may we say without disrespect? A kind of precipitate waddle with neither grace, fitness, nor dignity."

Women were gaining new skills and confidence. They demanded the right to vote. They wanted to elect people who would represent them on important issues, such as banning liquor in public places, or making laws to improve conditions for workers in factories and "sweatshops." Many women decided it was time to work actively to gain their rights as equals to men. And that included the right to participate in sports.

This wasn't a completely new idea. There was a call for women's suffrage, or their right to vote, in many other countries at that time. In 1909, a crowd of ten thousand women stormed the British Parliament in London. Many were arrested. Others went on hunger strikes to protest. A few years later, in 1913, ten thousand women marched in New York City to demand the vote. In Canada, women received the right to vote in federal elections in the year 1918. It would take another eleven years before women were declared "persons" under the law and were allowed to hold a seat in the Senate.

Bobbie was still young when all these events were happening, but everyone around her was talking about them. With her strength of will, her independence, and her naturally competitive nature, she became a perfect example of the "new woman."

3

High School
Athlete

Bobbie in her late teens. Her features have been highlighted to show up more clearly on the newsprint used in the 1920s.

As a young girl, Bobbie never cared about her looks. All she wanted to do was play sports. Not particularly tall or muscular, Bobbie was wiry, strong, and quick. She had dark, straight hair, an interesting, good-sized nose, a square jaw, and a strong neck. When she looked at you with her dark brown eyes, you knew this was a person who would be honest with you. She had a kind and generous nature, and everyone loved to be around her. She was often the life of the party, always making jokes and getting into mischief.

At home and at school, Bobbie found she could run, and run fast. With her parents' encouragement, she practiced every chance she could get – after school and on weekends. Bobbie

Barrie Collegiate Institute, shortly after it was completed in 1916.

ran lots of races against girls and won every race. By the time she entered grade nine at the new Barrie Collegiate Institute, people were saying she could run as fast as any boy. Most people thought that this just couldn't be true. They decided to have a race to find out, once and for all.

They chose the three fastest boy runners at the school for the 100-yard dash. Because she was a girl, the boys decided to be gracious and give her a three-yard head start. They figured they could easily catch up to her and win the race. They were wrong. Bobbie won by more than three yards. The whole school applauded her victory.

After that, Bobbie had trouble finding boys willing to race with her. She loved to win, but even more, she loved to compete. School team sports were a good outlet for her. She continued in athletics, leading her high school basketball team to a league title for Simcoe County. When she ran the 100-yard dash in the Great War Veterans Track and Field Meet in 1921, Bobbie was presented with her first track and field trophy.

In Canada, people used the British units of measurement – inches, feet, and yards – in the 1920s. But for international competition, the European metric system was used. Thus, one race in Canada was the 100-yard race, but in the Olympics, the 100-meter race was the closest equivalent (a yard is 0.9144 meters).

Bobbie was lucky to grow up when and where she did. Before 1913, the only physical education in Ontario schools consisted of calisthenics (exercises) and marching. But by the time Bobbie began school, sports had become a regular part of the school program, thirty minutes every day. She could participate with other girls in such sports as softball and basketball, a new game at the time.

The people of Barrie continued to be proud of Bobbie, even after she moved away. They considered her one of their own for her whole life. In 1967, just before her death, she was named the Marshal of the Barrie Winter Carnival and a fancy dinner was given in her honor.

In those days, it was difficult for women to find the right clothes to wear for sports. Some people believed it wasn't modest or ladylike to wear athletic clothes. In the early part of the century, many girls and women had to wear long skirts or "bloomers" when they played sports. Bobbie often borrowed her brother's shorts, her father's socks, and whatever T-shirt or jersey she managed to scrounge.

As Bobbie grew older, her mother didn't like to see Bobbie sweating and straining when she played. Sarah also worried her daughter would get hurt. Sometimes Bobbie had to sneak out of the house to train. She didn't have a coach to help her, either. There was no money to pay for one, and besides, most people didn't have private coaches in those early days of sport. But Max Rosenfeld encouraged Bobbie to practice and attended as

"We smilingly admit that our get-up wasn't exactly what fashion might decree – but what was a gal to do? With unflagging effort we tried all over town to purchase raiment in accordance with what the best-dressed sprinter was wearing, so that we could discard our modesty-preserving pup-tent bloomers, spinnaker middy and hip-length stockings. But girl athletes were as yet in the neophyte stage, and sporting goods houses proved an absolute blank … so we had to improvise our new and less blush-saving garments.… And anyway they got us there, even if they didn't exemplify the ultimate in art and good taste."

– Bobbie Rosenfeld, in her "Feminine Sports Reel" column in the *Globe and Mail*, January 6, 1940.

many games and races as he could. He usually had something to cheer about.

After the Great War Veterans Track and Field Meet in 1921, local sportswriters began to notice Bobbie, especially for her phenomenal ability to play ice hockey. One sportswriter described her play like this: "She checked hard and she had a shot like a bullet." Girls who played hockey were called "roughnecks" in those days. There was a lot of tripping, charging, shoving, and holding during games. To make matters worse, the players didn't wear helmets or shin pads. Many of them suffered cuts or bruises or more serious injuries. Lots of players lost teeth. Who knows? If Bobbie were playing hockey today, she might be in the National Hockey League or on the women's Olympic team. She was that good.

Bobbie and her family became Canadian citizens in 1920. What an important day that must have been for the Rosenfelds! Now they were truly Canadians. They had the right to live in the country, to vote, to pay taxes, and to participate in every aspect of Canadian life – including sports. Bobbie's parents had chosen Canada to make a better life for their children. As the future would show, they couldn't have made a better choice.

Harbord Collegiate Institute, in the early twentieth century.

4

A Move to the Big City

Bobbie yearned for more challenging competition. She had her eye on Harbord Collegiate in Toronto, which she had heard had an outstanding athletic department. Hoping to continue her schooling in Toronto, she failed two of her courses in her final year of high school in Barrie on purpose.

Meanwhile, the senior Rosenfelds were interested in moving to the big city as well. Many Jews from small towns moved to urban centers, such as Winnipeg, Montreal, or Toronto. Like most immigrants, they wanted to live closer to people with similar backgrounds and needs. They longed for a community that could provide them with the benefits of Jewish education, social gatherings, and burial – communal services that they had left

Top: *A Jewish butcher shop in Toronto in 1923.*
Bottom: *Immigrants in Kensington Market, a Toronto neighborhood that was mostly Jewish in the early twentieth century. This photo was taken in 1922.*

Left: Living conditions were difficult in Toronto's "Ward," a downtown neighborhood of mostly Jewish immigrants. *Right:* A billboard written in Yiddish in Toronto's Jewish quarter in 1917. The billboard lists ways people could send relief to Jews living in Poland, who were dealing with poverty and persecution at the time.

behind in the old world. They also wanted greater business and educational opportunities that only a large city could provide.

In 1922, the Rosenfeld family packed up their household and moved to Toronto.

The family managed to scrape together enough money to put a down payment on a house on Markham Street, well located in the new Jewish immigrant area and only a short walk to Harbord Collegiate. Though they wanted to support Bobbie's ambitions, their new location had advantages for the entire family.

Bobbie attended Harbord Collegiate for one year. During that year, she took part in a high school track and field meet at the Canadian National Exhibition (CNE). She led the Harbord women's track and field team to their first victory, again winning the 100-yard dash.

Harbord was a wonderful school for immigrant kids like Bobbie. Not only did it have excellent sports teams, but also other extracurricular activities such as the annual production of a Gilbert and Sullivan operetta. Most students thought Harbord was the best school in the province of Ontario.

Bobbie and her family moved to Toronto in the 1920s, a time when sports were becoming more popular, even within the Jewish community. Through sports, working-class immigrants might be accepted by the larger society. It was one way immigrant kids could "make good" and feel pride by excelling in sports and having their own team. Sometimes the team would join a league and compete with other teams in the league. To compete on an equal footing, each community needed its own space for training, practice, and meets.

In 1922, a new Jewish day school was built on Brunswick Avenue. This included a new sports facility.

Many graduates of Harbord Collegiate were successful and became well known:
o Comedians Johnny Wayne and Frank Shuster, who appeared regularly on television shows in Canada and the U.S. from the 1940s to the 1980s
o Sir Edward Beatty, first Canadian-born president of the Canadian Pacific Railway Company
o Dr. Charles Best, co-discoverer of insulin with Dr. Frederick Banting
o Charles Trick Currelly, the first director of the Royal Ontario Museum

Bobbie in her uniform with the letters of the Young Women's Hebrew Association proudly displayed next to the "T" for Toronto.

The building was to serve as the first Young Men's and Young Women's Hebrew Association (YM-YWHA, or "Y"). Jewish parents wanted to create a place of their own, where their children could play sports together in a familiar atmosphere. The result was a building and grounds to be used for practicing and playing team sports, such as baseball and basketball, as well as the ever popular wrestling and boxing. The "Y" was open to children and grown-ups, rich and poor, male and female.

Although much of the space at the "Y" was devoted to men's sports, some space was reserved for the women's teams. Bobbie joined the "Y" women's basketball team and played center position. In the 1920s, basketball was the fastest growing women's sport in Canada. Sometimes her team played against upper-class "Canadian" teams. Bobbie said that her basketball team from the Jewish "Y" came from "the other side of the tracks." The players were mostly poor young immigrants who had one thing in common: they loved sports. And this went a long way to victory.

Once, when her "Y" team came up against the established Toronto Ladies team for the first time, a miracle happened. The game took place in the gym at St. Christopher House, in downtown Toronto. It was a bitter, hard-playing match. First one team led the scoring, then the other. With the time almost up, Bobbie's teammate, Ann Kaplan, made a basket, giving the "Y" team a one-point lead. Only seconds remained in the game.

Then a forward for the Toronto Ladies, Athol Wesley, caught a pass just under the basket. She sent the ball up, up, up to the basketball hoop. It seemed that she would win the game for sure. But at that very second, everyone felt a vibration coming from the ground. It was just enough to make the ball miss the basket. A slight earthquake had occurred at the same second that Athol had made her shot! The "Y" team won that game, thanks to a freak of nature.

From 1915 to 1940, the Edmonton Grads dominated the field of women's basketball. During their existence, they won 502 games and lost only 20. They won 17 North American and Canadian championships. When they went to the Women's Olympics, they defeated all competition.

Even without miracles, the "Y" women's basketball team did well. In 1923, they won the Toronto championships and soon became Ontario champions. They were defeated only by the incomparable Edmonton Grads in the playoffs for the Canadian title.

5

Canada in the 1920s

Cars driving past Sunnyside Park, Toronto, in 1923.

The 1920s were a time when people with ambition, foresight, and luck could make fortunes. Some people got rich smuggling liquor into the United States, where it was against the law. But you could make money in legal ways, too. Gas stations and garages were built and roads were spreading out from the towns and cities. In 1914, there were 74,000 motor vehicles registered in Canada. By the time Bobbie got her first car in 1928, there were 1.19 million vehicles on the road. People who invested in producing and servicing these vehicles were quick to make money.

In 1925, Edward "Ted" Rogers invented a radio that ran on electricity. He called it the "Rogers Batteryless." People loved it because it produced a clearer sound than other radios. You could buy it for $250, a fairly high price, but a dollar down every week would eventually pay it off. Rogers became a wealthy man. His company, Rogers-Majestic Company, was the forerunner of what is now Rogers Communications.

People loved going to the movies to see their favorite stars, such as Douglas Fairbanks, Mary Pickford (from Toronto), and Charlie Chaplin. Together, these actors formed a new company called United Artists and made a fortune.

More opportunities were opening up for women. After all, they had proved they could do a "man's job" – hard labor in factories, mills, and mines – while most of the men were fighting overseas during the Great War. Women got jobs as teachers, nurses, telephone operators, and secretaries. A few women even became lawyers, doctors, or engineers.

For women, the 1920s were a time of liberation from many household tasks. Homemakers, like Bobbie's mother, Sarah, found work in the house was

- Dr. Maude Abbott (1869–1940) was a physician, researcher, educator, and a world authority on congenital heart defects.
- Mabel French (1881–1955) was a lawyer who gained the right to practice law in two different provinces.
- Elizabeth (Elsie) MacGill (1905–1980) was the first woman in Canada to receive an electrical engineering degree and the first woman in the world to become an aircraft designer.
- Carrie Matilda Derick (1862–1941) was a botanist and Canada's first female university professor.

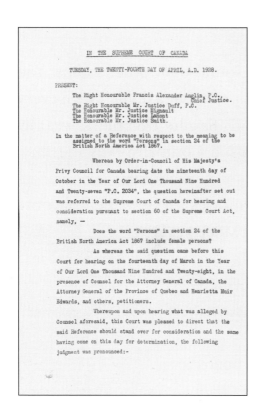

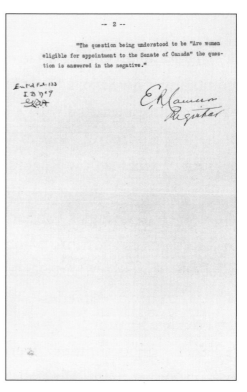

A document from the Supreme Court of Canada, dated April 24, 1928, stating that women are not allowed to run for Senate, because they are still not yet considered "persons."

According to British common law – then the ruling law of Canada – women were not "persons" and therefore could not hold public office. Suffragists Emily Murphy, Nellie McClung, Louise McKinney, Henrietta Muir Edwards and Irene Parlby fought to change this. Known as the "Famous Five," they presented a petition to the Supreme Court of Canada asking to be legally declared as "persons." The Supreme Court rejected their request. Undefeated, the Famous Five took the Persons Case to Canada's final court of appeal in London, England. In 1929, it was ruled that women were in fact persons and were therefore qualified to become members of the Canadian Senate.

getting easier all the time. If the family could afford them, she could take advantage of new labor-saving inventions like the vacuum cleaner, the washing machine, the electric mixer, the pop-up toaster, and the electric refrigerator. By now, many families in Canada had electricity, a telephone, and even indoor plumbing in their homes.

Between 1925 and 1928, life had become fast-paced. A lot of people had more time on their hands and were looking for ways to have fun. People loved to dance the Charleston and to listen to jazz music. In France, famous clothes designer Coco Chanel introduced the chemise dress, where the waist was low and the hemline high – all the way up to the knees. In England, writer A.A. Milne took his son to see a bear from Winnipeg at the London Zoo, and then wrote a wonderful book called *Winnie-the-Pooh*. People played miniature golf for the first time. And when they got tired of that, they tried to solve crossword puzzles, another popular new game. In 1926, Duke Ellington and Jelly Roll Morton cut the first phonograph records – before there were tapes or CDs. Al Jolson sang in the first "talkie" movie, *The Jazz Singer*. It put many silent movie stars, who didn't have good voices, out of work. And Mickey Mouse became a star with the release of *Steamboat Willie*, the first cartoon with sound.

Charles Lindbergh was the first person to fly from New York to Paris non-stop – an amazing feat for those days. It took him a little over thirty-three hours to complete the flight.

When people couldn't afford to drive a car, they could still take a train. A grand new Union Station opened in Toronto in 1927. It was the first place many immigrants saw when they arrived in Toronto by train. The largest and fanciest train station in Canada at that time, it had walls made of stone from Missouri and a floor of marble from Tennessee. The outside walls were built of Bedford limestone that shone in the sun. Each of the columns that decorated the outside walls weighed 75 tons and was 40 feet high.

In that same year, George Herman Ruth, whom everyone called Babe Ruth, led the Yankees in one of the greatest seasons in baseball history when he hit sixty home runs. It was a record that would stand for thirty-four years. But Babe Ruth wasn't a supporter of women in sports. He once said, "Women are too delicate. It would kill them to play ball every day." In fact, the 1920s would become the golden era of women in sports.

Facing page: By the lake at Sunnyside Park in Toronto, 1917.

The "All-Toronto" women's relay team (and managers). Left to right, Grace Conacher, Bobbie, Myrtle Cook, and Rosa Grosse.

6

The Complete Athlete

Bobbie played on many teams and in a variety of different sports. It soon became apparent to those who knew her that she was good at them all. She was an all-round athlete who loved to compete, regardless of the sport. With no professional training or coaching, she managed to excel by using her natural talents and working very hard. The complete athlete in all the sports she participated in, she always did her best to win for her team and herself. Soon she would be known outside her own circle as the champion who could do everything.

Track and Field

In the summer of 1923, Bobbie and her Hinde and Dauche

women's softball team (named after the Hinde and Dauche Paper Company) went to a picnic in Beaverton, a town on the east side of Lake Simcoe. An "open" race was advertised for any woman who wanted to run. Her teammates urged, "Why don't you go into the 100-yard dash?" Bobbie was embarrassed. She wasn't dressed for a race and was wearing bloomers – those long, puffy shorts – and old running shoes. Finally, her teammates persuaded her to enter the race.

"Ready? Set? Go!" The leading runner didn't seem to be working hard. She ran ahead easily and it looked as though she was a sure winner. Bobbie was trailing behind. But suddenly, near the end of the race, Bobbie had a tremendous burst of speed and won. What a surprise! People crowded around her. They were shouting, cheering, applauding. She met the distinguished-looking man who had organized the race. His name was Elwood Hughes and she found out that he was sports director of the Canadian National Exhibition (CNE), the biggest summer fair in Canada. He demanded, "Who is that girl?"

People asked Bobbie, "Do you know who you beat?" Bobbie had no idea.

They told her, "You beat Rosa Grosse, the Canadian champion!" Without knowing it, she had won a race against a famous track star. Up to that point, Bobbie had been an unknown outside her local teams. And here she had come within two-thirds of a second of the women's world record in the 100-yard race.

Above: *Bobbie (in white) and Rosa competing in the "Century Race" at the Canadian National Exhibition in 1923.* **Opposite page:** *The victorious "All-Toronto" relay team, left to right, Bobbie, Myrtle, Grace, and Rosa.*

It was an amazing feat for the young runner. Bobbie and Rosa would soon compete against each other again.

Thanks to that victory, Bobbie ran her first major track and field event at the CNE in August 1923. Billed as the "Century Race" for "ladies," it featured a strong group of runners. They included Bobbie, Rosa Grosse, Ann Miller, and the new American champion and record holder, Helen Filkey. The meet was called "international" because a team of women from the University of Chicago was coming to Toronto. The *Globe* reported that Tom Eck, the coach of the Chicago team, had brought his "fleet-footed lassies" to the CNE and expected to "clean up."

Bobbie won the 100-yard race to the roar of the excited crowd. She had equaled the world record of 11.0 seconds, finishing ahead of Grosse and Filkey. When Bobbie looked up from the finish line, she saw her father sitting on the stadium fence. Max Rosenfeld was banging on a piece of wood and shouting, "That's my girl, Fanny!" Bobbie's father was proud of his daughter's achievements and always encouraged her to do her best. He built a special cabinet for Bobbie's trophies and medals, and her mother polished them as if they were her best silver.

In the next race, instead of Bobbie racing against Rosa, she joined her, along with Myrtle Cook and Grace Conacher, in the "All-Toronto" relay team. Though they had never raced together before, they challenged the Chicago girls in the 400-yard relay. The Toronto team won with a time of 52.2 seconds. The coach of the Chicago team had to stop boasting.

Softball

The day wasn't over for Bobbie yet. Later that same afternoon, she headed further west along the shore of Lake Ontario to Sunnyside Stadium to join her softball team in their final game of the season. That year, for the first time, girls were allowed to play at the new stadium. By 1924, they would play three nights every week and earn a percentage of the receipts. They would even make enough money to buy decent uniforms and equipment!

Softball was a rough game. Only the catcher and the first basewoman wore mitts. There were plenty of broken fingers and lots of scrapes and bruises. Still, it was a favorite summer sport for many girls and women. Bobbie had a colorful way of talking about it. Once, when she described one of the girl pitchers on her "Y" team, she said, "Thelma [Golden] had a speed ball that came up to you the size of an aspirin tablet."

With Bobbie's help, her team won the City Championship over the favorites, the Toronto Athenaeums. More than 1,500

Women playing softball at Sunnyside Park. Throughout the 1920s and 1930s, these games drew large crowds.

people watched the two teams play. They said the women's game was even better than the men's!

Hockey

Hockey was Bobbie's favorite team sport. Bobbie began her Toronto hockey career on a bright February day in 1923. She was with a group of girls who were watching some skaters on Grenadier Pond in High Park. One very big girl, about six feet tall, bumped into Bobbie as she came around to where Bobbie was standing. Then she bumped into her a second time. When it happened a third time, Bobbie decided she wasn't going to take any more. She bumped the girl right back. They both started jostling each other about, so much that they broke through the ice!

Duke McCargy, the coach of the North Toronto AAA ladies ice hockey team, saw what had happened. He hauled them both off the ice. Later, he asked Bobbie to play for his team. When Bobbie showed up for the first practice, there was the girl with whom she had been fighting! Her name was Flo Preston, and they ended up being great teammates.

Before McCargy knew it, the team had made it to the Ontario finals. Although they lost to Ottawa in the final game with a score of six to two, the newspapers called Bobbie the outstanding player of the game.

Tennis

Next, Bobbie tried her hand at tennis. After playing for only one year, she won the Toronto Ladies Grass Courts tennis singles championship in 1924. But Bobbie didn't boast about her tennis achievement. She later said, "That was just an accident. I happened to be on one side of the nets when the final was being run off."

Constance Hennessy, one of the founding members of the Toronto Ladies Athletic Club, disagreed with Bobbie: "[Bobbie] didn't look powerful but, above all, she was aggressive. She simply went after everything with full force. She was just the complete athlete and she would have been good at any sport."

Bobbie on the softball field.

7

Working Girl

After Bobbie finished high school, like many other young women at that time, she took a course in shorthand and typing. In those days, letters were dictated to a secretary who would write them down in a fast, abbreviated way called "shorthand." The secretary would then transcribe her notes and type the letters using a manual typewriter.

Girls who worked in factories, stores, and offices formed teams that played after working hours. Most of them couldn't afford more expensive sports such as figure skating, golf, and tennis. But team sports such as hockey, basketball, track, and softball were sponsored by businesses and therefore available to all, rich or poor. Local factories and businesses often sponsored sports teams, because they could show civic pride, while at the same time advertising their name on team jerseys.

Patterson's Chocolate Company on Queen Street West in downtown Toronto was quick to offer Bobbie a job. The owner, Mr. Patterson, had read all about her in the newspapers, which often reported on local sports events. He knew she was a promising athlete and wanted her on his company's team. If Bobbie went to work as a secretary for Patterson's during the day, she could play on the team during evenings and weekends. The women's hockey team was called the "Pats" and Bobbie became its star player. The women played against other factory and company teams in the same league.

Bobbie, suited up for softball.

In the year 1925, on one glorious afternoon, Bobbie accomplished the unbelievable. Patterson's Athletic Club won the team title at the Ontario Ladies Track and Field Championship. It won gold in the 220-yard dash, the 100-yard low hurdles, shot put, discus, and the running broad jump. It won silver in the javelin and the 100-yard dash. The team had only three members, but Bobbie won all the prizes for her team. What was even more amazing was that Bobbie had never competed or been coached in the field

Miss Fanny Rosenfeld Makes New World's Record for 220 Yards

MARVELOUS WORK BY GIRL ATHLETE AT VARSITY STADIUM
The outstanding performances of Miss Fanny Rosenfeld were the feature at the ladies' meet at Varsity Stadium on Saturday. Miss Rosenfeld was timed in winning the 22-yard dash in 26 seconds. The previous world record was 26 2-5. Miss Rosenfeld also won the all-around championship by winning four firsts and two seconds for a total of 16 points. She is shown jumping and also in her brother's garments during intermission.

Above: *Bobbie made the papers after her outstanding performances at the Ontario Ladies Track and Field Championship. She is shown running, jumping, and, according to the caption, "in her brother's garments during intermission."*

Opposite page: *Bobbie with some of the many trophies and awards she won, even before the Olympics.*

events – discus, shot put, and javelin. People couldn't get over what an outstanding natural athlete she was. After Bobbie took home most of the trophies that day, the officials decided that in future track and field meets, one competitor would be allowed to enter only two track and three field events. Mr. Patterson got a lot of publicity for his candy factory that day.

Bobbie was getting ready for tougher competition. In just a few years, she would face her biggest challenge – the Summer Olympics of 1928.

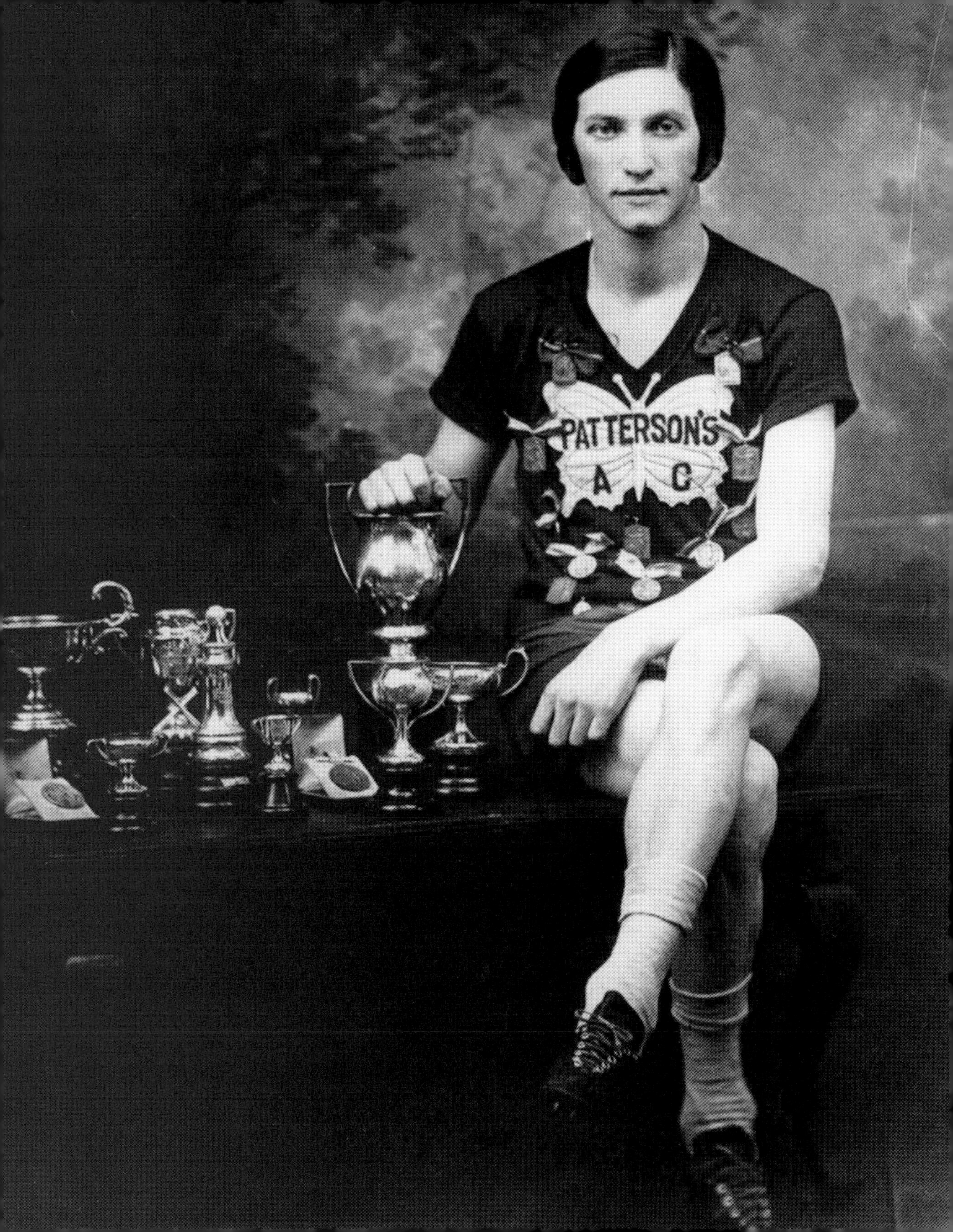
PATTERSON'S
A C

*The Globe was one of many papers to report
on the debate about women's participation
in Olympic track and field events.*

8

Women and the Olympics

The 1928 Olympics marked the first time women were allowed to compete in track and field. They had competed in other Olympic events in the past, such as swimming, sailing, and fencing. But track and field competitions were still thought to be too strenuous.

Baron Pierre de Coubertin, the man who started the modern Olympics in 1896, didn't believe women should compete at the Olympics in *any* sport. Coubertin believed that women's sports were against the "laws of nature." Invested in keeping women out of the Olympics, Coubertin proclaimed: "I personally am against the participation of women in public competitions, which does not mean that they should not participate in sports, yet not in public. At the Olympic Games, their primary role should be like in the ancient tournaments – the crowning of the [male] victors with laurels." Many agreed with him. Educators, doctors, and lawmakers – mostly male – still believed that women were fragile, if not inferior. A lot of women were ready to prove them wrong.

At the original Olympics in ancient Greece, women could be put to death for even watching the Games!

In Canada and the United States, young women at universities and colleges had been participating in sports, but only in a diluted way. They played by "girls' rules" on so-called "play days." Their coaches encouraged the young women to play for "play's sake," not necessarily to win. Competition was considered aggressive and unladylike. Often, scores of games weren't even recorded. Instead, the emphasis was on getting together after the games.

More serious women athletes joined athletic clubs and community centers to train and compete. These young women, like Bobbie, were not as worried about their "feminine" image. Some private sports clubs, like the Toronto Ladies Athletic

In response to the debate on women in the Olympics, a group of Toronto doctors wrote to the *Globe* early in the century: "The inclusion of women in the Games is impractical, uninteresting, unaesthetic, and we are not afraid to say, wrong."

Club, were founded by women for women only. Community centers and "Y's" provided a place where working-class people, both men and women, could practice and play. With more athletic facilities available to them, women could develop their skills in a variety of sports – including track and field.

Having won the right to vote, women in many countries felt a greater sense of responsibility. They wanted to make important social changes for the benefit of women and children. They hoped to improve conditions in the areas of health and education. Why not tackle changes in sports, as well? Women began to lobby for the right to enter into international competitions, such as the Olympics.

In France, there was a strong movement called the Fédération Sportive Féminine Internationale (FSFI) that advocated for women's athletics. Before the 1928 Olympics, the FSFI held two women's track and field meets.

By 1924, women were already competing in swimming, diving, golf, tennis, fencing, sailing, and archery at the Summer Olympics held in Paris. It was after the Paris Games that

A French sportswoman, Alice Milliat, formed the Fédération Sportive Féminine Internationale in 1922. In that year, the FSFI organized an international track and field meet in Paris. After 1928, when women were included in track and field events at the Olympics, the FSFI gradually lost power. The fourth and last Women's World Games took place in 1934.

Bobbie crouching to race, in her Patterson's Chocolate Company team uniform.

Coubertin resigned as head of the International Olympic Committee. Now was the chance for women to compete in Olympic track and field.

The Olympic Committee decided to give women this chance, but on a trial basis. At first, they promised the Fédération Sportive Féminine Internationale ten events, but they soon went back on their word. Women would be allowed to compete in only five track and field events at the 1928

Olympics – in contrast to the twenty-two track and field events for men. The women's events were the 100-meter race, the 800-meter race, the 400 (4 x 100) -meter relay race, the discus throwing event, and the running high jump competition. The British women's track and field team felt so betrayed that they refused to send their team at all. It was the first boycott of the Olympic Games, but not the last.

At the 1928 Olympic Games in Amsterdam, there were a total of 3,014 athletes – 2,724 men and 290 women competing in 109 events. Today, the proportion of men and women on Olympic teams is quite different. In the 2000 Games in Sydney, of the 10,651 athletes competing in 300 events, there were 6,582 men and 4,069 women.

The Canadian Olympic Committee decided to send a small women's team to participate in the track and field events. But which women were good enough athletes to represent Canada in the Olympics? The tryouts in Halifax, Nova Scotia, early in the summer of 1928, would decide that.

9

Halifax Olympic Tryouts

Myrtle Cook, Bobbie's former Toronto track teammate, became her Olympic teammate.

July 2, 1928. A crowd of five thousand people came out to the Halifax sports field called the Wanderers' Grounds. There were so many spectators that many people had to stand for over four hours. Great excitement was in the air as everyone waited for the women's sports events to begin.

The tryouts for the Canadian men's team took place in Hamilton, Ontario, on two days: June 30 and July 2, 1928. A number of Canadian records in track and field were broken and a strong team was selected: Percy Williams of Vancouver (100 meters and 200 meters), Phil Edwards of Hamilton (800 meters), and Jimmy Ball of Winnipeg (400 meters), to name just a few.

Although the International Olympic Committee had decided to allow only five track and field events, in order to make the meet more interesting the Halifax organizers scheduled other events as well. They added the javelin throw, the running broad jump, the 60-yard dash, and the 220-yard dash.

The competition for a spot on the Canadian Olympic women's team was fierce. The athletes who participated in the Halifax tryouts were very talented amateurs who had been playing sports all their lives. There were only six spots available on the women's team, because there wasn't enough money to send more athletes. At the tryouts, more than twenty-four women competed in fifteen events. They had all trained long and hard for this competition.

The competition in the 100-meter race was especially tough. Ethel Smith won the first heat, Myrtle Cook the second, and Bobbie the third. In the final race, Myrtle came in first with a record-breaking time of twelve seconds. The runners were so close that the referee had to reverse the decision of two of the judges! Because of their outstanding results, all three women were

Many Canadian records were set by women on July 2, 1928.
○ Ethel Catherwood, running high jump: 5 feet, 3 inches
○ Myrtle Cook, 100-meter race: 12 seconds
○ Bobbie Rosenfeld, running broad jump: 18 feet, 3 inches
○ Bobbie Rosenfeld, standing broad jump: 8 feet, 1 inch
○ Bobbie Rosenfeld, discus: 120 feet, 1 inch
○ Jean Thompson, 800-meter race: 2 minutes, 21 and 4/5 seconds

chosen to compete in the 100-meter race at the Olympics as well as another event, the 4 x 100 relay. Ethel Catherwood, from Saskatoon, Saskatchewan, broke all records in the running high jump event. Jean Thompson won the 800-meter race, while Jane Bell excelled in the 60-yard hurdles and the 100-meter race. They, too, were chosen to be on the Olympic team.

Besides being chosen as an Olympic team member, Bobbie had much to be proud of that day. She set three Canadian records, not broken until the 1950s. When she won the shot put, discus, and broad jump, and came second in the 100-meter race, one sportswriter called Bobbie "a whole team herself."

Nicknames were popular in those days. Ethel Catherwood was called the "Saskatoon Lily," Jean Thompson, the "Penetang Pansy," and Bobbie, of course, remained "Bobbie."

He added, "She was strong and jumped with a force that gave the male stars a thing or two to think over." At the end of the tryouts, she received the most points of any other athlete in Halifax – a total of seventeen.

In all, six women, including Bobbie, would participate in the track and field events at the Amsterdam Olympics. Myrtle Cook, a twenty-six-year-old secretary, and Ethel Smith, a twenty-one-year-old factory worker, represented the Canadian Ladies Athletic Club of Toronto. Jane Bell, an eighteen-year-old high school student, trained at Toronto's Parkdale Ladies Club. Twenty-year-old business school student, Ethel Catherwood, was originally from Saskatoon, but trained at the Parkdale Athletic Club before she went to the Olympics. And finally, Jean Thompson, the youngest member of the team, a seventeen-year-old high school student from Penetanguishene, Ontario, was trained by her high school coach.

Canadian and international sports reporters nicknamed these women the "Matchless Six." And this name remained with them for many years to come.

Olympic oath taken by women who competed at women's final Olympic trials in Halifax: "In the event of my being selected on the Canadian women's Olympic team, I solemnly promise that I will go to Europe with the team and that I will unconditionally obey both chaperone and manager until my return to Canada; also that I will put myself in the hands of the Canadian Olympic coach only; and that I will at all times conduct myself so as to uphold the honor of Canada."

10

Traveling to Amsterdam

The women track and field stars on the 1928 Canadian Olympic team inspired headlines even before leaving for the Games!

In total, there were seven women on the Canadian Olympic Team of 1928, six in track and field – the Matchless Six – and one in swimming, sixteen-year-old Dorothy Prior. The rest of Canada's team was made up of 109 men.

In proper perspective, this small team of seven Canadian women was drawn from a population of almost ten million. They were going to Amsterdam to compete against the cream of women athletes from twenty-one other countries. In Amsterdam, there would be a total of 121 women competitors in track and field, drawn from a combined general population of something like 300 million. Competing against the six Canadian women were twenty from the United States, nineteen from

Germany, fourteen from Belgium, and thirteen from France – to mention only the strongest.

International sports competition in a foreign country was a new experience for most of the young Canadians. Only one, Myrtle Cook, had been to an overseas match before. But Alexandrine "Alex" Gibb, the women's team manager, had great confidence in her small team, and so did Lou Marsh, a sportswriter from the *Toronto Daily Star* who accompanied the Canadian Olympic team. He called the women's team "the smallest, the cockiest, the best trained and the best organized Olympic contingent Canada ever sent forth."

Many Canadians were thrilled about women going to the Olympics to compete in track and field. A crowd of about five hundred people, including the mayor of Toronto, went to Toronto's Union Station to say good-bye to the team on that hot day of July 10, 1928. After all the speeches, Mayor McBride was so excited about the women's team that he kissed Ethel Catherwood on the cheek!

Although there was no television back in the 1920s, and radio was just starting to catch on, most people read the newspaper. Bobbie was already popular in Toronto because of her success in sports. People recognized her from the photographs in the Toronto newspapers like the *Globe* and the *Toronto Daily Star*. In addition to the seven women, the team had a manager, Alex Gibb, and a chaperone, Marie Parkes. The Canadian Olympic

Committee wanted to make sure these young women would behave properly and keep all the rules. Alex Gibb saw that they were well dressed and well behaved.

Alex Gibb and Marie Parkes had developed a love of sports when they were students at two Toronto private girls' schools – Havergal College and Branksome Hall. They both came from privileged upper-class backgrounds. The Matchless Six, on the other hand, included three students, two secretaries, and one factory worker. They had learned to play sports during evenings and weekends when their day jobs were over. Bobbie worked at Patterson's Chocolate Company to earn a living, before and after she went to the Olympics.

It hadn't been easy to find the money to send the team to Europe. Friends and relatives had worked together to raise money for the trip through bake sales, cutting grass, and even a minstrel show at Massey Hall. After many delays, the Ontario government finally gave the Olympic team ten thousand dollars to help with expenses.

The team took a train from Toronto to Montreal and then boarded a ship that would take ten days to reach Southampton, England. From there, they had to make their way to Amsterdam in the Netherlands. There was no such thing as flying to Amsterdam in eight hours, as we do nowadays. It was Bobbie's first trip across the Atlantic since she had arrived in Canada as a baby. She would remember the experience for the rest of her life.

On the train to Montreal, the manager of athletics for the Canadian team, Bobby Robinson, called a special meeting of the women's team. He had discovered that some of the women had been drinking soda pop a few days before! He scolded them: "You can't win a relay on pop. From now on, the girls will be in strict training and will be expected to live up to the schedule the same as the men." He knew that soda had too much sugar and was bad for the athletes' training. They passed the time on the train singing songs like "Button Up Your Overcoat" and playing the ukulele, a popular musical instrument in the 1920s.

They finally arrived in Montreal late at night. After a few hurried speeches by the mayor of Montreal and other important people, the tired athletes made their way onto the ship. It had been arranged that all the track and field athletes, swimmers, wrestlers, and oarsmen would take the ship called the S.S. *Albertic*, while the boxers, cyclists, and lacrosse team would follow one week later on the *Empress of Scotland*. Finally, at four o'clock in the morning, the *Albertic* steamed out of Montreal harbor on the way to Europe.

It wasn't all fun and games during the trip. The athletes had to follow a tight schedule. They got up at eight in the morning for a salt-water bath, had breakfast at nine, and then worked out for one-and-a-half hours. The four women from the relay team weren't used to running together and needed to practice

Canada's female Olympic athletes wave good-bye from the train, at the beginning of the long journey to Amsterdam in 1928. Bobbie is third from the right, in the white cap. (The photo has become cracked over the years.)

passing the baton. In the afternoon, they took a three-mile walk on the ship, ate dinner at six, and went to bed at ten. Years later, Jane Bell told the story about dancing late one night and sneaking to bed after curfew. She knew she would have gotten into big trouble if she had been found out.

Alexandrine Gibb said of this group: "Girls are high strung at any time. But girl athletes who are at the peak of their condition for the contests are about as safe to handle as a basket full of dynamite."

Bobbie wasn't ready to explode, but she certainly had a quick sense of humor. A newspaper headline read: "Fanny, Brilliant in Repartee as she is on Sports Field." The article continued: "She kept the ship party in a continual roar with her funny sayings and doings." For example, one of the male athletes, Brant Little, stepped up to Bobbie as she was going up to the ship's deck. Teasing, he asked, "Ticklish, Bobbie?" She answered promptly, "No, Jewish."

Bobbie also loved playing poker with the boys on the ship and kept everyone laughing with her jokes and wisecracks. The story is told that when the team was about to leave for Amsterdam, someone shook hands with Bobbie and said, "Bring home the bacon!" Bobbie turned towards the person, gestured with her palms up, and grinned. She said, "Vat? Me? Bacon?" Of course, she was joking about the fact that many Jewish people don't eat pork.

No coach accompanied the women's team to the Olympics. But the Canadians helped each other out. For example, Phil Edwards, the sensational 800-meter runner, helped Jean Thompson with her training. Bobby Kerr, captain of the men's team, led the women in their morning workouts on the ship. And manager Bobby Robinson kept an eye on everyone.

The team finally arrived safely in Amsterdam. It was time to prepare for the opening ceremonies.

Alexandrine Gibb was a strong promoter of women's sports in Canada. She advocated the idea of "girls' sports run by girls." By that, she meant that women should organize, coach, referee, and play sports without the interference of men. Gibb and a group of other women started the Women's Amateur Athletic Federation of Canada (WAAF) and she became its first president in 1925.

A poster for the 1928 Olympic Games.

II

Opening Ceremonies

In the early days of the Olympics, there was no such thing as an "Olympic Village" where athletes from all countries ate, slept, and relaxed. (This was created for the first time at the 1932 Games in Los Angeles.) Each country had to make its own arrangements for its athletes. The Canadian men's team stayed in a little rundown hotel called the Holland Hotel, while the women boarded in a rooming house far from the Olympic stadium.

As well as practicing every day, the women had time for fun. They joked that one way they worked out was running after the streetcars. Not to get a ride, but to mail their letters! Mailboxes in Amsterdam were on the backs of the streetcars, and the women ran after the streetcars to mail their letters and postcards.

During a break from their training, the women decided to hire a driver who would take them around the city with his horse and carriage. Since none of them spoke Dutch, they had a hard time communicating with the driver. Bobbie had an idea. She tried out her Yiddish, the language she spoke at home, since it sounded more like Dutch than English did. It turned out that the driver was also Jewish and understood her perfectly. Pretty soon, she had talked him into letting her take the reins. The excited Bobbie drove up and down the canals and over the bridges of Amsterdam, proud that she wasn't afraid to talk to anyone.

Motto of the Olympic Games: "Citius, Altius, Fortius" (Faster, Higher, Stronger)

The official opening ceremonies of the Ninth Olympiad took place on Saturday, July 28, 1928. Though the day began with a steady downpour of rain, the sky started to clear around noon. Prince Henry of the Netherlands arrived at 1:45 p.m. and entered the royal box. Military and marine bands played the Dutch national anthem, while 1,200 singers from all over the Netherlands sang to the music. The flags of all the participating nations flew in the breeze. As the Olympic flag was raised to a blast of trumpets and roar of cannon, 35,000 people watched from the stands. Suddenly a flock of pigeons was released, flying in all directions above the crowd. There were forty-six pigeons, each representing one of the competing nations.

The Olympic flag was first introduced during the 1920 Summer Olympics in Antwerp, Belgium. On the flag are five interlocking rings, three above and two below, representing the five major continents. At least one of each of the colors – blue, yellow, black, green, and red – is on the flag of every country in the world.

Then the procession of the nations began. Led by the representatives of Greece – because it was in Greece where the Olympics first began about 2,500 years before – over three thousand athletes walked briskly around the track. They saluted the prince as they passed the royal box. The multicolored uniforms of the athletes looked like a rainbow on the huge playing field. The Dutch team from the host country was the last group to march in front of the royal box. This order of the march of athletes has continued to the present day.

At the head of the Canadian team, rower Joe Wright Jr. carried the flag and Earl McGrady, a strong wrestler from Regina, carried the heavy sign with "CANADA" printed in large letters. Behind them marched the Canadian athletes and officials, three across in thirty-five rows. The women looked very striking in their red hats and shoes, pleated white skirts, silk blouses, and

It was quite a feat to build the Olympic stadium in Amsterdam, the city of canals, where the ground was wet and marshy. About 4,500 piles had to be driven into the soft ground. The surface was raised six feet (1.8 meters) and about one million cubic yards (764,600 cubic meters) of sand were used to fill in the ground.

white jackets trimmed with red. The men were handsome, too. Once in a while, someone would break out in applause or shout "Canada!" Then the

women would wave back at their fans. It was all part of the fun. The serious part, the Games themselves, would soon begin.

This was still a relatively new modern Olympics and for this reason there were a number of firsts, besides the fact that women were competing in track and field. It was the first time the Olympic flame burned throughout the Games and the first time a large board was set up to show the results of the events. As we shall see, it would also be the first time in modern Olympic history there would be a dispute about the results of a women's track and field race.

Olympic Oath: "In the name of all competitors, I promise that we shall take part in these Olympic Games, respecting and abiding by the rules which govern them, in the true spirit of sportsmanship, for the glory of sport and the honor of our teams."

Bobbie (left) and Betty Robinson at the finish line.

12

Winner of the 100-Meter Race

When Bobbie was chosen for the Canadian Olympic team, it was for the discus event in particular. She had, after all, set a Canadian record for the discus at the tryouts in Halifax. Knowing that she was good at many sports, the Canadian officials were confident she could win an Olympic medal, whatever the event.

However, the discus throw was scheduled on the same day, July 31, as the final 100-meter race. This important race would decide who was the fastest woman on the planet. With all the preliminary races, Bobbie just didn't have the time or the energy to compete in both events. In the end, the Canadian officials decided that, with all her experience, Bobbie would have the best chance for a medal in the 100-meter race.

One hundred meters is not a long distance – about the length of a football or soccer field. To race the 100 meters, an athlete needs both speed and power. It's not an endurance race, but one that's more like an explosion where the tiniest fraction of a second mustn't be wasted.

Among the women racing against Bobbie were her two teammates, Myrtle Cook and Ethel Smith, Elizabeth (Betty) Robinson from the United States, and two runners from Germany, Leni Schmidt and Ern Steinberg.

All the runners were keyed up, like thoroughbred horses before a race. Sometimes this can mean trouble. Canadian Myrtle Cook and German Leni Schmidt started ahead of the gun – once together and then individually. Both had two false starts. According to Olympic rules, they were disqualified before the race began.

The discus throw from which Bobbie withdrew in order to run the 100-meter race was won by Halina Konopacka of Poland, who threw the discus about 128 feet. At the Olympic trials in Halifax, Bobbie had thrown it 120 feet.

Crying her heart out, Myrtle sat down on the grass. For over half an hour, her head was buried in her arms and her body was shaking with sobs. She was the holder of the world record for the 100 meters and wasn't allowed to race! It was a bitter disappointment that she would remember her whole life. Bobbie didn't think it was fair. She even tried to argue with the starting official, but it did no good.

The German competitor, Leni Schmidt, showed her disappointment by shaking her fist under the starter's nose. The official backed away a step or two and then ordered her off the track. He was not pleased about the way things had started. Later, he was criticized so much for the way he had disqualified the women that he ended up resigning from the Olympic staff.

Only four runners were left – Bobbie, Ethel Smith, Betty Robinson, and Ern Steinberg. Finally, on the fourth try, the race began for real. Ethel and Bobbie were so nervous now that they were slow on the getaway. Betty Robinson began with a good lead. Bobbie trailed behind until the halfway point of the race. That's when she gave it everything she had! One reporter wrote, "She rallied strongly and raced down the stretch, probably faster than any woman ever traveled in the world." And when the tape broke, the race was so close it was hard to tell who had come first – Bobbie or Betty.

Ethel finished in third place for a bronze medal and Ern Steinberg came in fourth. But to this day, people are still arguing about who came first. At that time, there was no automatic "photo finish" to check the results of a race. The only photos we have of the race are unclear. The five judges had to use their eyes, their hand-held watches, and their experience to decide the winner.

Two judges thought Robinson had broken the tape with her arms. Others disagreed. That would have disqualified her immediately and given Bobbie the gold. Even if Betty had run

Top: Bobbie winning her semi-final heat in the 100-meter race. Ethel Smith is just behind her on the left. *Bottom:* Bobbie (left) and Betty Robinson (just to her right) reach the tape at the same instant in the 100-meter final. Ethel Smith, who placed third, is on the far right.

fairly, people still weren't sure about who came first. The English and French judges said that Bobbie had won, but the one German and two American judges voted for Robinson. That made two against three. In the end, the judges gave the gold to Robinson and the silver to Bobbie.

Alex Gibb, the manager of the women's team, wanted to protest. She had the support of P. J. Mulqueen of the Canadian Olympic Committee and Bobby Robinson, the manager of the men's track and field team. The three walked over to the judges' stand and handed in a written protest. But Dr. A.S. Lamb, Chair of the Canadian Olympic Committee and President of the Amateur Athletic Union of Canada, refused to support the protest. Lamb thought it was "unsporting" to complain.

A lot of people agreed with him. One reporter for the Toronto *Globe* wrote, "Protests are not popular in this country, where athletes know how to win and also how to lose." After all, the Olympic ideal was to play the game for its own sake. Taking part was supposed to be more important than winning.

In the end, Betty Robinson's victory stood. The women on the Canadian team were furious. A short time after the 1928 Olympics, the women had another reason to be angry with Dr. Lamb. He voted against *all* women participating in the Olympics. Fortunately, he was outvoted. In December 1928, Dr. Lamb was forced to resign as President of the Amateur Athletic Union of Canada.

Bobbie had made the American work hard for her gold medal. Betty Robinson equaled her own world record of 12.2 seconds for the 100-meter race that day. Bobbie had run the race in 12.3 seconds. What was Bobbie's reaction? She made a joke! She said that if she had won a gold medal, she would have been given a synagogue when she got back to Toronto. With the silver medal, all she would get was a pew. Bobbie was gracious and no one ever heard her complain again about the results of that race.

In later years, when a reporter asked Bobbie what her most satisfying accomplishment was, she said, "When I defeated Betty Robinson … by five yards in the relay at the Millrose Games in New York." Bobbie was fair, but she *did* love to win.

The Millrose Games is an annual track and field meet where athletes from all over the United States come to compete. It is called the "Nation's Greatest Indoor Track Meet" and continues to the present day. In 1927, Bobbie's relay team won gold at the Millrose Games.

After the Olympics, in February 1929, the U.S. officials invited the Canadian Olympic champions – Bobbie, Myrtle Cook, Jane Bell, and Ethel Smith – to compete in the 4 x 100 relay race. They came in second, although Bobbie was ahead of Betty Robinson in her section of the race.

13

The Good Sport

Jean Thompson competing in the 800-meters in Amsterdam.

Sometimes when athletes push themselves too hard, they get injured. That's what happened to Jean Thompson while she was training for the 800-meter race in Amsterdam. She pulled a tendon and had to rest for a week before the race. Banking on her for the middle-distance race, the Canadian team officials worried about how Jean would compete with her leg injury.

The 800-meter race would be a hard one to keep up. It was close to half a mile – about eight times the length of a football field. The team managers knew that Jean could run well, even with her injury. But they were concerned about her confidence. So they made an unusual decision. They decided to enter Bobbie in the race, too. They figured that Bobbie could give Jean some moral support for this very tough race.

Bobbie had never trained for this event. She was used to shorter distances like the 100-meter and 200-meter races. But the officials persuaded Bobbie to try out for the preliminary heats. Wanting to help her team and Canada, she agreed. To no one's great surprise, Bobbie managed to qualify. She would join Jean in the final 800-meter race.

A crowd of fifty thousand people was watching in the stadium on the afternoon of August 2. The spectators knew they were in for an exciting race. The gun went off and nine runners sprang away from the starting line. During the first lap, Jean Thompson stayed in second place behind Kinuye Hitomi of Japan. But Jean gradually began to fall behind to third place and then to fourth. She was running easily, reassured with Bobbie right behind her. She was getting ready to put on her usual burst of speed for the last 100 meters.

Just then, Hitomi decided to move ahead, too. The Japanese runner accidentally bumped Jean. This had never happened to Jean in a race before. She was so startled that she veered off to another lane and began to slow down.

Bobbie had been running last in the race the whole time, keeping an eye on Jean. She could tell something was wrong. Maybe she saw a change of rhythm or a change in the way Jean was running. Maybe she noticed that Jean was in the wrong lane. Whatever the reason, when she saw what was happening, Bobbie put on a burst of speed and caught up with Jean. For the rest of the race, Bobbie kept talking to her teammate: "Don't give up," and "You can make it." With Bobbie's words in her ears, Jean kept running, right to the end of the race.

Many people were convinced that Bobbie could have moved up further, and maybe even won a medal. But Bobbie made the choice to stay back and let Jean come in ahead of her. Bobbie felt it was more important to help her teammate, as she had been asked to do. At the end of the race, Jean Thompson came in fourth, earning three points for the Canadian team. Even Bobbie earned two points for her fifth place standing. Lina Radke of Germany won the race with a world record time of 2 minutes, 16.8 seconds. Jean and Bobbie were only one second short of matching Lina Radke's record.

The spectators were more impressed with Bobbie than if she had won a medal. Such generous behavior is unusual in sports, where winning is usually the most important goal.

Alexandrine Gibb was to write later that year: "Bobbie Rosenfeld's sportsmanship in this event was one of the high spots of the games. In the annals of women's athletics, there is no finer deed than this."

However, there was a bad side to the results of the 800-meter race for women. When they had finished the strenuous race, the women threw themselves down on the infield. *The New York Times* newspaper reported it like this: "At the finish, six of the runners were completely exhausted and fell headlong to the ground. Eleven wretched women were strewn upon the cinder track." It was just the proof some male officials and reporters had been looking for that the event was too difficult for women. No one mentioned that many men who had competed in the 800-meter race fell to the ground with exhaustion when *they* finished the race!

At their next meeting, the all-male International Amateur Athletic Federation had a vote. With pressure from Pierre de Coubertin and the Pope in Rome, they decided to remove the 800-meter race for women from the next Olympics. They were so successful that the event did not return to the Games until 1960. Why did the IAAF make this decision? Perhaps it was out of genuine, though mistaken, concern for women's well being. But some people thought it was done to show women athletes that men still had the power to make decisions over them.

Through the years, various sports have been added to and subtracted from the women's roster of Olympic events. At the 2000 Olympics in Sydney, Australia, for example, new events for women included the hammer throw, the pole vault, and the triathlon.

Later, when Bobbie became a sports journalist, she championed women's rights to compete in "strenuous" sports. In an article she wrote in *Chatelaine* magazine, Bobbie said: "The modern girl is a better worker and a happier woman by reason of the healthy pleasure she takes in tennis, hockey, lacrosse, swimming, running, jumping and other sports."

The 400-meter relay team – Jane Bell, Myrtle Cook, Ethel Smith, and Bobbie.

14

The Matchless Six

Sunday, August 5, 1928. It was the final day of the Olympic track and field games and Canadian hopes were running high for the 400-meter [4 x 100] relay race. The Canadian team for this event would be made up of Bobbie, who would run the first leg, Ethel Smith, Jane Bell, and Myrtle Cook, who would finish off.

The four women came out onto the field. To stay warm, they had wrapped themselves in bright red Hudson's Bay blankets. Ethel and Myrtle had cut off the short sleeves of their team jerseys, but the large red maple leaf still showed plainly on the front. The women did a few leg stretches to warm up. The pressure was especially intense because of the previous controversial race, in which Myrtle had been disqualified and Bobbie had come in second. For this final event, the runners longed for the gold, not so much for themselves but for Canada.

Carrying their respective team's baton, Myrtle Cook from Canada, Betty Robinson from the United States, and Leni Schmidt from Germany would be running the anchor, or the final leg of the race. Who would be the fastest?

Before the race could begin, the teams had to pick from a hat to decide which lanes they would run. When the officials arrived, Bobbie made a flying dive to get into the hat first. When she saw she had drawn the number for the inside lane – considered the best spot – she jumped up and down with excitement and held her hand high in the air with her index finger pointing. The Canadians were having good luck, at last. The women hugged each other and took their separate positions on the track.

But the race didn't start smoothly. A split second before the gun went off, Bobbie broke. The runners were called back and Bobbie was given a warning. Would this be a repeat of what had happened to Myrtle in the 100-meters? The crowd was quiet. Once again, the first runners took their positions. The starting pistol went off and this time it was a clean start. Bobbie was a good two meters ahead when she handed the baton to Ethel Smith.

Ethel grabbed the baton and tore down the back course with her clothing and her hair flying back in the wind. Jane turned to look back at Ethel and began sprinting. Ethel slapped that solid baton into Jane's palm. She had spread the lead a bit more. That's when Jane Bell ran the race of her life. By the time she had rounded the final curve and straightened out to hand the baton to Myrtle, the Canadians were leading by about three meters.

Jane Bell later recalled, "Of all the things that have happened to me in my life, many good things, I don't think I was ever as proud and as thrilled as when I stood and saw our flag going up, and took a look and saw the four of us with tears."

Here's where the race was almost lost. While Jane was running at full speed, Myrtle had to start running too so that no time would be lost during the exchange of the baton. Myrtle had only ten meters within which to accelerate and get the baton. This exchange had to be timed to the split second. Myrtle was almost out of the passing zone when Jane handed her the baton – at the very last possible second!

Now Myrtle showed why she had been chosen for the team. She was running against Betty Robinson, the sixteen-year-old from Illinois who had won the gold in the 100-meters. Myrtle had something to prove. She crossed the finish line five meters ahead of Robinson. The Canadian women had set a new world record of 48.4 seconds, breaking the one they had made the day before by a full second.

When she realized she had won, Myrtle jumped up and down for joy. Then Bobbie, Ethel, and Jane ran up to her, jumping as well. They kept hugging each other and laughing. They were moving around so much that the photographers had trouble keeping them still for the official pictures.

The Canadian flag – at that time, the red ensign with the Union Jack – was raised on the center masthead to show the entire world that the Canadian relay team had won. The young women mounted the podium to accept the gold. They cried with happiness as they heard Canada's national anthem. It was a glorious moment for the four women and for all of Canada.

Ethel Catherwood competing in the high jump at the 1928 Olympics. She won the gold medal in the event.

Later that day, when Ethel Catherwood won the gold in the high jump by clearing 5 feet and 1 inch, everyone knew the ~~1.59 meters (5.2 feet)~~ Matchless Six were true champions. The small but mighty team of six women had earned two gold, one silver, and one bronze medal, along with a fourth- and fifth-place finish. With twenty-six points, Canada led the overall women's score. The United States, with its larger team of nineteen women, came second with twenty points.

That night, the women went out to a dance club to celebrate. Someone told the orchestra leader about the team's victories and the band kept playing "The Maple Leaf Forever." Bobbie didn't mind. She would have been glad to hear those lyrics all night long:

Here may it wave,
Our boast, our pride,
And join in love together,
The thistle, shamrock, rose entwined,
The Maple Leaf forever.

The Canadian women's team had rightly been named the Matchless Six. No Canadian Olympic track and field team since – men or women – has been able to do what they did during one unforgettable week in the summer of 1928. As for Bobbie, she won thirteen points – more points than any other woman. In fact, she won more points for her country than any other competitor, man or woman, at the 1928 Olympics.

The Matchless Six:
Bobbie, Jean, Ethel
Smith, Myrtle, Ethel
Catherwood, and Jane
(with chaperone).

What happened to the other women of the Matchless Six?

○ Jane Bell (Doane) became a physical education teacher. She married and had two children. When she retired, she moved to Myrtle Beach, South Carolina, and passed away in 1998 in Fort Myers, Florida.

○ Ethel Catherwood suffered an injury during the Canadian championships in 1931. She never competed again. After two marriages and divorces, she died in 1987 in California. Until recently, her gold medal was the only individual gold medal ever won by a Canadian woman in track and field.

○ Myrtle Cook (McGowan) married, had two sons, and became a sportswriter for the *Montreal Star*. She coached Hilda Strike, who won silver medals in the 100-meter and 4 x 100-meter relay at the 1932 Olympics. She was active in sports organizations like the Toronto Canadian Ladies Athletic Club and the Mercury Athletic Club in Montreal. She was also on the British Empire/Commonwealth Games Committee and the Olympic Committee from 1932 to 1972. She died in 1985.

○ Ethel Smith (Stewart) married, had a baby, and stopped competing in sports. She died in 1979.

○ Jean Thompson withdrew from sports competition on the advice of her coach, who said there was nothing more to strive for. She got married, had one daughter, and died in 1976.

15

A Triumphant Return

People continued to shower Bobbie with gifts ... including this leather cabinet made to hold Bobbie's medals. Her Olympic medals are on either side of the engraved center plate, which reads, "Presented to Miss "Bobby" Rosenfeld by the Jewish Community Baseball League."

Before going back home, the girls participated in several exhibition meets in France and England. Since the British women's team hadn't gone to the Olympics, it was a good opportunity to give everyone a chance to compete. Besides, people wanted to see the great Canadian women athletes in action. After their voyage home (during which the girls were allowed to drink soda pop), the Matchless Six arrived in Montreal.

The Montreal city officials gave them a big welcome. They were given a tour of the city and a big banquet. The mayor of Montreal and other important people gave speeches and each athlete was given a silver powder compact. Bobbie said, "All I can say is that we are proud of what we have done for Canada,

The "Matchless Six" with their chaperone and manager at the victory celebration back in Toronto. Bobbie is the second woman from the right.

and we hope to do even better next time." But that was nothing compared to what was awaiting them in Toronto.

When they arrived at Toronto's Union Station on August 28, a crowd of more than 200,000 fans greeted them – almost half the city's 570,000 population. The six young women climbed down from their special train onto the platform. They were dressed in the beautiful outfits they had worn at the opening ceremonies of the Olympics. When the crowd saw they had arrived, people started cheering and threw their hats up in the air. Many tried to shake the hands of the returning heroes.

Lyrics for "See the Conquering Hero Comes":
See, the conqu'ring hero comes,
Sound the trumpets, beat the drums.
Sports prepare, the laurel bring,
Songs of triumph to him sing;
Sports prepare, the laurel bring,
Songs of triumph to him sing.

When the girls walked down to the lower concourse, the band played "See the Conquering Hero Comes" and "The Maple Leaf Forever."

When the young sports stars walked out to Front Street, the band played the popular marching tunes of the day. That's when the crowd went wild! The noise was deafening as thousands of people cheered and shouted at the top of their lungs.

To celebrate, a four-mile procession through the city had been organized from the train station to Sunnyside Park. Mayor McBride appeared in the first open car, with the girls following in the next two. The carriage of the National Ladies' Club, drawn by a team of nine gray horses, followed the cars. The band of the Queen's Rangers and the Police Pipers played and marched behind the carriage. Next followed the members of all the sports clubs in Toronto. Almost every sporting club and organization in the city had decorated a car or a float. Along the entire route, people cheered and cars honked. Hundreds of children stood along the sidewalks watching the parade march by. The sirens from the Parkdale fire station added to the commotion. All this for the returning Olympic heroes!

How proud and excited the young women felt, sitting in their open cars at the head of the procession! Bobbie loved the spectacle. She recognized many familiar faces along the way. Talkative as ever, Bobbie had a response for every cheer. People ran into the road, wanting to get closer to the athletes. When shy Ethel Catherwood complained about the slowdown, Bobbie said it was fine with her. As far as she was concerned, it could last forever. This was the applause she had been dreaming about all her life.

When the parade went by Patterson's Chocolate Company, Bobbie's fellow workers cheered from every window and waved long white and green streamers in her honor. Some of the workers came out and handed the women boxes of chocolates. What did they do? They threw the chocolates to the children running alongside their car, to the newspapermen coming along behind, and to the mounted police keeping order along the route. The parade lasted about one-and-a-half hours until it reached Sunny-side Park at nine in the evening.

Another 100,000 admirers were waiting for the Olympic champions when they arrived at Sunnyside Park. The athletes struggled through the crowd to line up on the platform as people started singing "See Them Smiling Just Now." One of the newspaper reporters said, "Nobody kissed Ethel Catherwood, although a hundred looked as if they would like to." Now the women were so overwhelmed, they couldn't speak. Then, all together, they answered the crowd with the yell of the Olympic team and with "Canada, Canada, Canada – C-A-N-A-D-A – Canada!"

After greetings from George Ferguson, the premier of Ontario, each member of the Matchless Six was called upon to make a speech. Of course, Bobbie's was the longest: "It was awfully nice to make the team. It was awfully nice to look forward to the trip. But it was nicest of all to look forward to coming home. If my English is not very good now, please remember we have been in foreign countries. We did not go over for individual honor, but to bring the Canadian flag to the top of the pole." At the end of the speeches and cheers, each woman received a sterling silver tea set as a token of the city's appreciation.

But that wasn't all. The Junior Council of Jewish Women honored Bobbie with a fancy tea party in the Blue Room of the King Edward Hotel. More than a hundred of Bobbie's friends

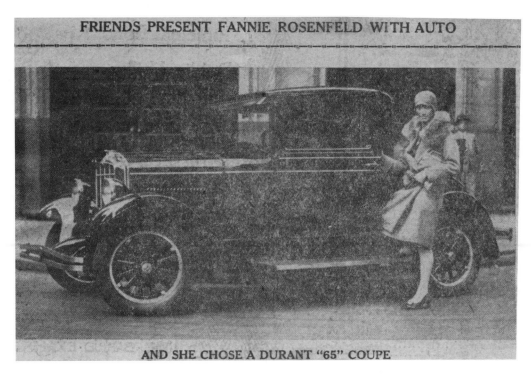

FRIENDS PRESENT FANNIE ROSENFELD WITH AUTO

AND SHE CHOSE A DURANT "65" COUPE

A snappily-dressed Bobbie with her new car.

and admirers attended the celebration. They were proud of her as someone from their community who had become a celebrity. In recognition of her achievements, Bobbie was presented with a car – a Durant sports coupe. What an extraordinary luxury for a working woman in those days!

When the car salesman asked Bobbie if she could drive, she assured him she could. But when she sat behind the steering wheel for the first time and let go of the clutch, the car almost jumped onto the sidewalk. The truth was that Bobbie had never driven a car before. A small thing like that wouldn't have bothered the new Olympic champion!

Bobbie in uniform for the Pats, her hockey team.

16

A Cruel Blow

In 1929, Bobbie announced that she would stop running. This was the way she put it: "I think I've done enough running for one person." However, she was still the star defensive player for her basketball team, center for her hockey team, and first base for her softball team. The reasons for her decision aren't clear. Maybe it was because she loved team sports more than track and field, and continuing with both was too much. Or perhaps she was starting to feel the pains in her joints that would eventually become part of her illness.

Soon she would have no choice. She would be forced to stop playing sports completely. Within a year after coming back from the Olympics, Bobbie was stricken with a chronic illness called arthritis.

How did this happen to Bobbie? Some people think she played too many sports, too hard, and in too short a time. It is true that she always pushed herself to the limit and often beyond. It is also true that she never did have a coach to help her train properly. More likely, though, she would have gotten this condition anyway. Even today, no one knows for sure what causes arthritis. There is no known cure.

Whatever the reason, Bobbie suffered tremendous pain and fatigue. Today, there are many treatments available to help people deal with arthritis. These include medical drugs, massage, exercise, and relaxation techniques. There are specialists and physiotherapists who deal specifically with arthritis. But in those days, there were very few treatments. Bobbie was told to stay in bed, apply ice packs, and take Aspirin every day. She kept up this routine for eight months.

What is arthritis? Arthritis is a disease that causes the white blood cells in the body to attack the cartilage. Cartilage acts like a cushion to protect the bones in joints like the ankles, knees, hips, and elbows. When one has arthritis, everything hurts. It's hard to get out of bed in the morning, to do up buttons, to write, to dress, to climb stairs, or even to get up from a chair.

The doctors were desperate to help her. Some even suggested amputating the foot that was causing her so much pain. But how could they amputate the foot of the most famous woman athlete in Canada? She, her mother, and the family doctor refused. Her mother promised to nurse Bobbie back to health at home, and she did.

Bobbie felt angry, frustrated, and cheated. She was only twenty-five years old. She was at the prime of her athletic career. She had reached the top of her sport as an Olympic medallist. And now, even the slightest movement gave her pain. As she lay in bed during those long months, she felt the world was passing her by. She was afraid she might never walk again, let alone play sports. She didn't know if she could continue to work and make a living to support herself.

AURA LEE HOCKEYISTS LOSE TO PATTERSONS

"Fanny" Rosenfeld Returns to Game and Shows Flashes of Former Ability

Led by the one and only "Bobby" Rosenfeld, who took part in her first athletic contest since her long layoff owing to illness. Pattersons' Pats defeated Aura.

Years later, Bobbie alluded to how she felt during this time in her life. "If you've ever known sickness – if you have ever known a helplessness that holds your spirit immobile...." She was speaking from experience and from the heart.

Fortunately, Bobbie wasn't the sort of person who gave up. After months of complete bed rest at home, Bobbie started to walk on crutches. She was told to stay on those crutches for one year. Slowly, she began to go outside again. One day, in March 1930, she even went to watch her hockey team, the Pats, play.

It was just before the last period. The Pats were losing the game. Bobbie just *had* to help her team out. She threw her crutches aside, put on the green, white, and gold uniform, laced

REPLACES CANE WITH STICK
The patrons of the Pats-Aura Lee girls' hockey game at Varsity Arena early last evening were given a real

Above and opposite page: Local newspapers excitedly reported Bobbie's return to hockey.

up a pair of skates, and went out on the ice. And, of course, she ended up scoring the winning goal for her team. That's how much Bobbie loved to play!

Doctors who have heard this story said it was a near-miracle that she had been able to play at all. Her mother was in a state of shock when she heard about the game. Bobbie just shrugged. She had hidden the newspaper articles about the event from her family.

In the 1931-2 season, Bobbie was named the outstanding player in the Ontario Women's Hockey League. But her arthritis struck another blow in 1933. After she recovered from that bout, Bobbie never played with a sports team again – not softball, basketball, nor hockey. Nor did she ever again play individual sports like track and field or tennis. For the rest of her life, she often used a cane to help her walk. By 1935, her participation in sports was over.

17

Searching for a New Life

Irene Storey (Weber) shares a place of honor with Bobbie in the Barrie Sports Hall of Fame.

After her first lengthy bout of illness, Bobbie knew she wouldn't be able to play sports the way she had before. She had to find new ways of using her energy – ways that would be less hard on her body. Needless to say, she couldn't keep away from sports. For a while, she tried her hand at coaching and managing teams. She already had some experience. In the summer of 1930, Bobbie had managed her softball team, the Maple Leafs.

She had also coached individuals, such as Irene Storey (Weber), a young athlete from her old hometown of Barrie. Irene became the national champion in the 60-meter and 100-yard dashes, and the Canadian record holder in the 220-yard dash. She also won the junior gold medal in the 60-meter race at the British Empire Games of 1930.

In 1931, Bobbie coached a women's hockey team, the Toronto Pals, and took them to Madison Square Garden in New York City to play against the New York Wolverettes. She also managed a basketball team called Langley's Lakesides. They too went to Madison Square Garden, where they played an exhibition game in front of 14,000 fans.

Bobbie volunteered her time to amateur sports associations. In 1932, she was vice-president of the Olympic Ladies' Softball League and the Ontario Women's Softball Association. She was also secretary and later president of the Ladies' Ontario Hockey Association.

Why did Bobbie stop coaching? In those days, there was little money for sports, especially women's sports. Coaching was a volunteer job that did not pay. And Bobbie needed to make a living. Her continuing problems with arthritis also limited her role as a coach. She suffered from pain and fatigue for the rest of her life. Arthritis is the kind of disease that is unpredictable. Sometimes a person feels better, other times worse. Since she never knew in advance how she would feel, Bobbie didn't want to let the team down. It was hard enough to keep working at her regular job when she didn't feel well.

With physical activity no longer at the center of her life, Bobbie needed to find a new career for herself. She had had enough of her work as a secretary at Patterson's Chocolate Company. In 1932, she was offered a job to write a sports column for the *Montreal Herald*. She decided to give that a try. The *Herald* was a popular paper that covered local news. It concentrated on social events, crime, and sports. Bobbie worked for a sports editor called Elmer Ferguson (Fergy), who wrote a popular sports column. Fergy had himself been a well-known Canadian runner.

In those days, Montreal was the largest city in Canada with a population of 600,000. Like Toronto, it became a city of immigrants from many countries.

Still unwilling to give up sports altogether, Bobbie played softball for Muncy's Ladies' Team in Montreal and basketball for a women's team from the Montreal YM-YWHA. She even became president of the Women's Softball Union of Quebec.

In all, Bobbie stayed in Montreal for only three months. Maybe she missed Toronto or her family. Maybe the job wasn't quite what she expected or the pay wasn't very good. Maybe she left because in Quebec sportswriters were not allowed to play sports. Whatever the reason, she decided to move back to Toronto.

Still looking for a suitable job, Bobbie got a position selling insurance for the London Life Insurance Company in 1934. As always, she worked hard at it. She got so good at her job that, after a year, she became a supervisor – the only woman in Canada to hold such a high position at that time.

Finally, in 1937, the Toronto *Globe and Mail* hired her as a sportswriter. The newspaper was growing. By that time, it had a daily circulation of about 100,000. The publisher, George McCullagh, was a major sports fan who owned part of Maple Leaf Gardens. He was especially fond of hockey, football, and horse racing. McCullagh liked the idea of having a celebrity, a famous athlete like Bobbie, in his sports department.

The Toronto *Globe* became the *Globe and Mail* in 1936.

Bobbie had finally found another niche for herself. She was happy to be able to carry her love of sports into a new field. She was also relieved to know that she could make her own living. Still, for the rest of her life, whenever anyone asked Bobbie for her autograph, she signed it, "Just a natural … Bobbie." She never forgot her days of glory in sports.

Bloor Street, Toronto, in 1930.

18

Canada in the 1930s

Some historians say that the 1930s was the worst decade of the twentieth century. In 1929, the stock market crashed in the United States. It wiped out many people's savings in just a few days. By the end of 1930, nearly five million Americans were unemployed and more than 26,000 businesses had gone under. Canadians were also deeply affected. By 1932, one quarter of Canada's labor force was out of work. The world economy went into a nosedive called the Great Depression.

It seemed that even nature was against the people. There was no rain for long periods of time and water became scarce in the midwestern farmland of Canada and the United States. The topsoil blew away, and nothing would grow. People lost

The Depression caused hardships across the country. Here, men eat at a Montreal soup kitchen in 1931.

their farms and started to travel all over the country, looking for food, work, and a new place to live.

The most ominous of all the events of the 1930s was the rise of dictatorships. There were certain governments in the world that didn't care about democracy and basic human rights. The dictators in Germany, Italy, Spain, and Japan took away people's right to speak freely, to practice their religion, to vote for whomever they wanted, and much more. They were prepared to kill or imprison masses of people in order to gain and keep power.

In 1933, Adolf Hitler with his National Socialist Party, the Nazis, came to power in Germany. In 1935, the Nuremberg Laws took away German citizenship from Jewish people. In 1937, the Nazis targeted the churches. Thousands of Catholic and Protestant clergy were arrested and placed in the first concentration camp, Buchenwald. Many prisoners were beaten, starved, and worked like slaves.

On November 9, 1938, during one frenzied night of looting and destruction, the Nazi storm troopers attacked Jewish homes, businesses, and synagogues. This night was called "Kristallnacht" or the Night of Broken Glass. When it was over, ninety-one Jewish people had been murdered and many more had been beaten up or arrested. On September 1, 1939, Germany invaded Poland. Soon after, Britain and France declared war on Germany. By the end of the decade, World War II had begun.

How Bobbie must have felt about these events, we can only imagine. She probably attended the rally on November 20, 1938, at Maple Leaf Gardens. Over twenty thousand people came out to protest the persecution of Jews in Germany.

Still, Canada wouldn't change its newly tightened immigration policy. The doors to Canada were now shut. Between 1933 and 1945, Canada accepted less than five thousand Jews. The Jews of Europe were mostly left to their fate – terrible suffering and death.

The anti-Nazi rally at Maple Leaf Gardens had the support of several important politicians. The new mayor of Toronto, Ralph Day, as well as Canada's first woman member of Parliament, Agnes Macphail, addressed the crowd.

The 1930s were a horrific time for Jews in Europe, but it wasn't always comfortable being Jewish in Canada, either. World events had increased anti-Semitism – hostility toward Jews – even in Canada. Jewish people couldn't buy land in some areas, or move into certain neighborhoods. Many golf, tennis, curling, and sailing clubs did not allow Jews to join. Some hotels and resorts had signs that said "No Jews Allowed" or "Christians Only."

On a summer day in August 1933, a riot at Christie Pits in downtown Toronto broke out. It happened during a baseball game. A group of Nazi supporters called the Pit Gang brought baseball bats and lead pipes to the park. They were ready to beat up any Jews they found there. They raised a banner painted with a huge swastika and started to shout, "Heil Hitler!"

TORONTO   **OTTAWA**   **MONTREAL**

CANADIAN LABOR PRESS

WORKERS OF CANADA
REPUDIATE RACE INTOLERANCE!

Use Your Efforts as Members of the Labor Movement to
Promote Freedom for Every Individual irrespective of race
or creed, to Secure Peace and Happiness in the Dominion

Oppose Anti-Jewish Feeling

PROTEST WITH ALL YOUR MIGHT AGAINST ANY
ATTEMPT TO PROMOTE HITLERISM IN CANADA

In several places throughout the Dominion recently, attempts have been made to create prejudice against the Jewish people in these cities upon the lines of the policies laid down by the National Social Party of Germany under Adolph Hitler. So far the movement seems to have been instigated by ill-advised young people of the community who evidently ignorant of British and Canadian traditions, imagine that they can take the law into their own hands to discriminate against any race, creed or section of the population. The Workers of Canada must take a firm stand against such suggested or contemplated unchristian race intolerance and use all their influence to aid the lawfully constituted authorities in preserving peace and freedom for every section of the community.

If the Anti-Jewish feeling is allowed to spread, it may extend to other racial and religious groups, and finally lead to lives being lost, property destroyed, and thus tarnish the well deserved reputation of Canada as leading the Nations of the World in the principles of liberty, equality and brotherhood of man.

The Workers of Ontario and throughout Canada know that Jewish Workers form in many cases strong support for the International trade Union Movement and that they have always been willing to take their share in the struggles for better wages and conditions. It would be an everlasting disgrace to the Canadian Workers if they allowed their Jewish, or any other fellow members of the community to be vilified and discriminated against by ill-advised young people; therefore it is the duty of the Canadian Workers to protest with all the power at their command to the lawfully constituted authorities against any further spread of this unchristian anti-Jewish feeling.

An anti-racism poster put out by the Canadian Labor Press, *in response to growing anti-Semitism in Canada during the 1930s.*

About two hundred Jewish boys ran forward and chased them out of the park. When other young Jews heard about the trouble at Christie Pits, they met at the "Y" on Brunswick Avenue. Volunteers in trucks drove them to the park. By then, the fighting had spread to the surrounding streets. Shops were broken into. Jews were beaten up. The violence lasted for about six hours until the police finally stopped it. By the end of the riot, the Jewish boys had managed to grab the Nazi banner and tear it to shreds.

What happened to the bullies who had attacked the Jews in the park? They weren't charged. The judge said it had only been a joke. But the Jewish community in Toronto knew the situation was far from funny.

It was unfortunate that the 1936 Summer Olympic Games had been planned to take place in Berlin, Germany. Though Pierre de Coubertin had insisted that the Olympics be separated from politics, Hitler, now leader of Nazi Germany, used the Berlin Olympics to promote his Nazi ideas. The result was that many athletic organizations, such as the workers' sports movements, boycotted the Games that year. They knew that Jewish athletes in Germany were being persecuted and Jewish sports clubs had been shut down.

Many Canadian Jewish athletes decided to stay away from the Olympics. They included boxer Sammy Luftspring, race walker Henry Cieman, and speed skater Frank Stack. As for the

The 1930s weren't all doom and gloom. Some exciting new developments:

○ The first World Cup soccer tournament was played in Uruguay in 1930.

○ Ritz crackers and 7-Up were introduced in 1933.

○ The ballpoint pen was invented in 1938.

○ Two classic children's books were published: *The Story of Babar*, written by Jean de Brunhoff, in 1931, and *Mary Poppins*, by Pamela Travers, in 1934.

○ Canadians Joe Shuster and Jerry Siegel created the comic book hero, Superman, in 1938.

America

○ BINGO became popular and so did Monopoly, the game people said would never take off because it took too long to play.

Canadian media, except for Bobbie at the *Globe and Mail* and a sports editor for the *Vancouver Sun*, almost no one understood what the fuss was all about. They would find out soon enough.

In 1930s Canada, radio sports broadcasts became very popular. Especially when Foster Hewitt announced the play-by-play action from Maple Leaf Gardens in Toronto. "He shoots! He scores!" became as Canadian as the maple leaf. Even Bobbie tried her hand at radio sports. In December of 1930, she began announcing the play-by-play action of women's basketball games for Toronto radio station CFCA. Foster Hewitt said of Bobbie, "She is quick and humorous and has a particularly good line of patter that should keep her listeners interested as well as well informed."

19

The End of an Era

A hockey game in progress at Maple Leaf Gardens in Toronto, November 1931.

Even during the Depression, sports were still popular. You could pay your fifty cents or one dollar and forget your worries in the excitement of a game. People came out to watch their favorite hockey, baseball, and football teams. They gambled on horse racing in the hope of making some money. Making money had become an issue in sports, as well.

In the 1930s, many so-called "amateur" athletes played baseball, hockey, and football for money and other perks. The sportswriters called them "shamateurs." However, an amateur was someone who participated in sports for the love of it, without earning any money. In those days, amateur athletes, like Bobbie, believed that sports should be played for sports' sake.

It was a time when amateur athletes had little coaching and paid their own expenses. They made many sacrifices in order to play the sports they loved.

From the beginning of the Olympics, the ideal of "amateur" sports had been a source of controversy. Coubertin and the early organizers demanded that athletes be free from outside influence and political pressure. This meant that Olympic athletes had to be rich enough to pay for their own travel and other expenses. Many athletes thought it was hypocritical to expect them to train and make sacrifices for an ideal that was designed only for rich, upper-class men.

Today, the definition of "amateur" is different. Most amateur athletes pursue their sport full-time, receive excellent coaching, and get grants from the government or athletic scholarships from schools. Since 1982, "amateur" athletes are allowed to accept prizes in money and gifts. With the emphasis on superstars, many successful athletes are signed up to endorse sporting equipment, clothing, or even food and drinks.

Because she had to work to support herself for her entire life, Bobbie might have been bitter about not having made money from her heyday in sports. Her sister Ethel Berman has said, "If Bobbie had participated in sports today, she'd be a millionaire with all the endorsements athletes have now." Though she believed in amateur sports, Bobbie joked about how the women athletes in the 1920s had been "babes in the woods," naïve about their amateur standing. She described how an exhibition race had been organized in Barrie, her former hometown, right after the Olympics. When Bobbie arrived, she found that no other women had shown up. So, once again, Bobbie raced against the men. Of course, she won. What was her prize? A lampshade and one yard of ribbon!

New technological changes had major effects on sports during the 1930s. Artificial ice was being used for inside rinks. Floodlights were installed for games such as baseball, football, and soccer. More indoor facilities were built all over the country with gymnasiums, swimming pools, running tracks, and arenas. Athletes could now train all year long, without worrying about the season or the weather. These facilities were especially built for professional teams, who also received the best equipment from sponsors. The emphasis now was on the men's professional teams in baseball, hockey, and football. This was where the money went. Even in the depths of the Depression, a brand new Maple Leaf Gardens was built in Toronto. About fifteen thousand people came out to see the first hockey game played at the Gardens in 1931.

"Hockey Night in Canada" was all about *men's* hockey. No one paid much attention to outstanding women's teams like the Preston Rivulettes or the Edmonton Grads anymore. Small businesses could no longer afford to sponsor women's sports and big business was too busy backing professional men's

Maple Leaf Gardens under construction, September 21, 1931.

The End of an Era

teams. Women who wanted to train and compete often had to use outdoor facilities or indoor facilities at off-hours.

Because times were hard and so many men had lost their jobs, there was a lot of pressure for women to stay at home and leave the few existing jobs to the men. These ideas spread to the area of women's sports. Conservative attitudes about women's sports became common again. Even Agnes Wayman, the female president of the American Physical Education Association, declared, "There is a widespread agreement that girls should not be exposed to extremes of fatigue or strain either emotional or physical."

Even those male sportswriters who supported women's athletics often wrote about how a woman could participate in sports and still stay "feminine." They praised the "good" sports, like figure skating, golf, and tennis. They ignored the "bad" ones that were more aggressive and rugged. Some male sportswriters went even further. One columnist for the *Vancouver Sun* called female athletes "leathery-faced Amazons with flat chests and bony limbs."

Girls were no longer encouraged to play in sports that required strength, speed, and muscle power, like the track and field, ice hockey, and softball of Bobbie's glory days. Women who participated in these team sports were considered too "masculine." The golden age of women's sports had become dull and tarnished.

Bobbie in the late 1930s.

20

Career Woman

Though Bobbie could no longer play the rugged sports she loved, she continued to support women in athletics. She fought against sexism in sports her whole life, first as an athlete and later as a sportswriter.

Never rich, Bobbie lived in a crowded house on Markham Street in Toronto during the 1930s, with her father, mother, and her three sisters. Each sister had a paying job. Gertie worked as a secretary, Mary as a bookkeeper, and Ethel as a stenographer. Their father, Max, had worked as a salesman for the Ontario Coal, Coke and Wood Company since his arrival in Toronto. Times were tough but manageable for the Rosenfeld family. Everyone contributed to the household and shared expenses.

The house on Markham Street, where the Rosenfelds lived for many years, as it looks today.

At a time when women were "queens of the household," Bobbie was in an unusual situation. Most young women were expected to get married and become housewives and mothers, while their husbands were the breadwinners. This would never be the case for Bobbie, who stayed single, childless, and financially independent her whole life.

Bobbie had never made a fuss about marriage. When she was twenty years old, she had joked, "I'm going to put the names of all the fellows in a hat and draw one. If I get a butcher, that's who I'll marry. If I draw the baker, all well and good. But I hope I don't get a sprinter, because I don't want to spend my time running after him." Unconventional as always, Bobbie never chose to marry. Instead she chose a career. She became a sportswriter.

Bobbie wasn't the only woman sportswriter at that time. She was in good company. Alexandrine Gibb had been writing for the

Bobbie often helped out at events such as the Canadian National Exhibition, where she could be found selling cheeseburgers. The papers noted, "This is no ordinary bark- er for the husky-voiced vendor is a lady – Bobbie to the crowds but to her many fans, better known as Bobbie Rosenfeld, Sports Reel columnist on the Globe and Mail.*"*

Toronto Daily Star since 1928. Myrtle Cook of the Matchless Six was writing for the *Montreal Star*. Another athlete turned sportswriter, Phyllis Griffiths, worked for the *Toronto Telegram*. These women sports journalists had been successful athletes, coaches, or administrators in their younger years. They brought a female slant to sports reporting. They also made sure that women's sports would be reported fairly.

Before these women came on the scene, only men wrote about sports in the newspapers. They wrote mostly about men's professional sports. Women's sports got only a small fraction of the coverage – about five percent – and then usually about figure skating, golf, and tennis.

In 1937, Bobbie began a column called "Sports Reel" in the *Globe and Mail*. In it she covered all kinds of sports – from softball, basketball, hockey, curling, and track and field to bowling and rodeo riding. She covered women's sports everywhere – in Ontario, in Canada, in the United States, and around the world. But mostly, she loved to write about the local sports scene in Toronto. Sometimes, her column discussed a specific sport or one particular theme. Other times, she filled it with snippets about different sports events and sports personalities, including her personal compliments, complaints, and observations to the public. She wrote in a very personal way, engaging her readers to follow her columns on a daily basis. She kept this up for twenty years.

When Bobbie began her column, journalism was very different from what it is today. Her research entailed talking on the phone to people about local happenings in women's sports. Otherwise, she got the news from other newspapers or from national news services like the Canadian Press. She wrote down the information in shorthand. Then she typed her column on a manual typewriter, getting it ready for the editor who was rushing to meet a deadline. The early edition of the paper had to hit the streets by ten in the evening. Sports fans liked to pick up the *Globe and Mail* to check on the results of horse racing and afternoon sports games. The *Globe and Mail* was the morning newspaper in Toronto. It competed with the afternoon papers, the *Toronto Daily Star* and the *Toronto Telegram*.

Bobbie worked in a new downtown building called the W. H. Wright Building at the corner of King and York Streets. The building was one of the first in those days to have its own cafeteria. She enjoyed talking to other reporters during her lunch hour, and sharing gossip and news with them. From home, she could get there easily with two streetcars. Sometimes she drove her car to work.

She started with a salary of about thirty dollars per week. That wasn't too bad, considering the Depression was still hitting people hard in the late 1930s. You could go to a movie for twenty-five cents and buy a full-course meal for one dollar.

Covering women's sports was different from men's sports.

Unlike many male reporters, Bobbie didn't visit teams at baseball spring training or travel long distances to see the Toronto Maple Leafs at the Stanley Cup playoffs. She didn't interview players in the dressing rooms or on the playing field. Because of her bad arthritis, Bobbie could not travel easily. She had back problems from the arthritis and often used a cane. Then there was also the fact that reporting on women's sports had less prestige, less advertising dollars, and therefore less funding. In many ways Bobbie's job was tame compared to that of her male counterparts. She wasn't part of the hard drinking, hard talking, late night crowd. Bobbie's day was more a regular nine-to-five job.

Gord Walker, a veteran *Globe and Mail* sportswriter who knew Bobbie well, described her: "Bobbie never bragged about her achievements in sports. She brought class to an otherwise all-male department."

In 1950, when journalist Robert Fulford first came to work at the *Globe and Mail* as a young man, there were about fifteen writers in the sports department, only one of them a woman. Fulford remembers that Bobbie was treated like "one of the boys." Everyone treated her fairly and with respect. One day, Bobbie said to Fulford about one of his stories, "You really got that!" The compliment meant a lot to him. It showed that she was still generous, this time to a rookie reporter.

Bobbie's column as it appeared in the late 1930s.

21

"Sports Reel"

Why was Bobbie's column, "Sports Reel," so important? Bobbie used her column to stand up for women's rights in all areas, not only in sports. She called remarks against women "the same old malarkey" – nonsense. In a 1933 article for *Chatelaine* magazine, Bobbie wrote: "The girl athletes have successfully crashed the sacred sanctum of men's sport realms. The sporting public likes them and wants them. They have been an attraction on many a sport programme, frequently taking all the curtain calls and 'stealing the show.' Would all this ballyhoo of leathery limbs, flat chests, [and] physical injury be a direct result of male resentment to the female intrusion of their athletic circle?"

Bobbie's column was called "Feminine Sports Reel" until 1942, when it was shortened to "Sports Reel."

"Feminine Sports Reel," January 10, 1941, the *Globe and Mail.*

One of those periodic diatribes against Eve has burst into print again. Its author is Jack Miley, chivalrous two-fisted scribbler with the New York Post … It's the same old malarkey flavoring most all misogynistic articles levelled at women athletes. Just in case you're not familiar with the trend of thought, we print typical paragraphs:

"A female's flushed face over a hot stove is not only prettier but more practical than a purple face produced by puffing and panting from participation in some masculine sport for which nature never intended her.

"Women's place is in the home, and I never saw a girl yet who didn't look a sight better with a frying pan than a tennis racquet."

And more about girl athletes' legs looking like turkey gobblers' and the fact that girls in sport never get any place.

Why these gentleman of the press insist on taking a few cobwebby tales about women competitors, giving them new twists and endowing them with universality and delivering them as proof that women are physically, mentally, and morally unfit to traverse the field of sport with their boy scout brothers beats us.

What is more beautiful in sport than this: Colored ice surface, a blazing beam of light spotlighting the whirling figure of a human doll, spinning in rhythmic perfection, effortless, without strain, a symphony of grace.

What is more beautiful in sport than a graceful figure poised atop a high diving board, leaning forward, arms arched, and floating off into space, coming down to the water like a great sea bird, a thing of infinite grace, striking smoothly, without a splash, and streaking into the depths, leaving hardly a ripple?

Or watching Alice Marble gliding over tennis courts, or the sight of some graceful girl golfer swing with precise rhythm and a certain power on a teed-up ball.…

Bobbie reminded people that events were always happening in women's sports, as well as in men's. Whether it was softball or tennis, skating or skiing, Bobbie covered it all. She had her favorites, of course, like hockey and softball. But she tried to be fair and write about any sports events she thought might be of interest to her readers.

Bobbie encouraged girls to participate in sports in schools and clubs. She pushed women to keep fit and healthy through sports: "This column holds that sports competition, when properly organized and directed, has a contribution to make to the education of women."

Bobbie wanted women to have greater opportunities in all sports. She supported women's roles as umpires, referees, coaches, and officials. In her columns, she gave many examples of female coaches and trainers in such diverse sports as horse racing, golf, swimming, tennis, and boxing. Bobbie mentioned women athletes by their name and by their team so that they would be recognized by the public. She wrote about their grace, rhythm, and intelligence – as well as their strength and endurance. And always, she praised their accomplishments.

In some of her more serious writing, Bobbie discussed the legal and political implications within women's sports and how these affected all women. She also wrote about women in society and women's contribution to the war effort. She wrote about the greed and corruption that had regrettably become

SPORTS REEL
by BOBBIE ROSENFELD

I MUST CONFESS that the work-
ings of the large brains in amateur

The conductor of this column is
as outraged at the latest attempt

May 28, 1941
"With all due respect to the estima-
ble teachers of physical education,
this column holds that sports competition, when properly organized and
directed, has a contribution to make to
the education of women, and that it is
the responsibility of women teachers of
physical education to offer a program
that will make this contribution to girls
who are athletically skilled."

January 7, 1950
"Mere Male will, of course, advance
with that [old] argument that women
lack aptitude and ability for sports
tasks like being an umpire or a referee.
This theory of course, indicates only
a warped ego of a bunch of males and
calls for a flat contradiction."

part of professional sports. She encouraged the improvement of sports facilities for both men and women. For example, in one column she complained, "How in the world is basketball going to get to be one of the top customer attractions here if there is no place to put the paying customer?"

Although Bobbie's columns were about sports, they were not *only* about sports. During the twenty years Bobbie wrote her column, she battled tough opponents – apathy, prejudice, and greed. But most of all, she never gave up trying to help women gain recognition in sports.

22

Canada in the 1940s and 1950s

Women factory workers soldering fuse boxes at a munitions plant during World War II.

While Bobbie was busy with her writing career at the *Globe and Mail*, the world was embroiled in World War II. By the time it was over in 1945, 15 million military people and about 35 million civilians had died. Countless people had lost their homes and property. Cities and towns all over Europe were totally destroyed – bombed, burned, gutted. Even on this side of the ocean, Canada had lost over forty thousand people, mostly soldiers, in the struggle to keep the world "safe for democracy."

Just as in World War I, women did their part by working at such jobs as drivers, secretaries, mechanics, and factory workers during the conflict. Of course, when the war ended, they were laid off again to make room for the returning men.

Entertainment in the 1940s:
- Walt Disney released *Pinocchio* and *Fantasia* in 1940.
- New cartoon characters like Sylvester the Cat and Tom and Jerry appeared for the first time.
- People hummed the tunes of popular songs like "Somewhere Over the Rainbow" or "White Christmas" from the movies.

Entertainment in the 1950s:
- The *TV Guide* magazine would help you find new TV shows like "I Love Lucy."
- Or you could read new comic strips called "Peanuts" and "Dennis the Menace."
- Popular new tunes included "Frosty the Snowman," "The Doggie in the Window," and "Purple People Eater."
- Or you could play with hula hoops or Barbie dolls.

In spite of the war, people still loved to watch sports – just as they had during World War I. On April 18, 1942, the Toronto Maple Leafs defeated the Detroit Red Wings, four games to three, to win the Stanley Cup before a record crowd of 16,200 at Maple Leaf Gardens. Maurice "Rocket" Richard of the Montreal Canadiens scored fifty goals in fifty games – a new NHL record – in 1945.

The World Series celebrated its fortieth birthday in 1943. Since there was a shortage of male players, the All-American Girls' Baseball League was founded that year. Ten percent of its members were Canadian women who went down to the

United States to play. People still wanted to watch baseball games, even if it was women who were playing. After all, young women were encouraged to stay fit and healthy for the war effort. Sometimes women's sports teams raised money or entertained the soldiers. At the height of their popularity, the women's games attracted more than one million spectators per year.

When the soldiers came home, many went back to school. Most got married and started new families. The first "mother's allowance" checks arrived in 1945, just in time for the mini-population explosion. The "boom" was not only in babies, but also in the sale of new houses, furniture, cars, and appliances. The television suddenly became the hottest item that people wanted to own. In 1948, ninety percent of Canadian homes had radios, while fifty percent had telephones. After the sacrifices of the war years, everyone was looking forward to a better, more prosperous life.

The year 1944 saw Canada's first Racial Discrimination Act. It banned the publication or display of any expression of racial or religious discrimination. In 1948, the United Nations adopted the Universal Declaration of Human Rights. But Black people and Jewish people were still not allowed to own property in certain places, and Ontario laws made sure people abided by those rules. Finally, in 1950, the Supreme Court of Canada overturned this unfair ruling. (Canada would finally get serious about human rights when the government created the Charter of Rights and Freedoms in 1982.)

People had had enough excitement during the 1940s and wanted to settle down to a quiet life. The 1950s became a decade of stability and "normalcy." But the 1950s weren't completely dull. There was another war, called an "action," in Korea, where some Canadian soldiers fought (and died) under the flag of the United Nations. A new kind of music called "rock 'n' roll" came on the scene. When Elvis Presley visited Toronto in 1957, twenty-four thousand screaming teenagers filled Maple Leaf Gardens.

The 1950s were also a frightening time. A crippling virus called polio was on the rampage. Children were told not to go to public swimming pools or play with their friends at parks and playgrounds. In 1953 alone, over eight thousand people, many of them children, got polio. Some died, but many were disabled for life. Finally, in 1954, Dr. Jonas Salk developed a vaccine that would prevent this dreaded disease.

New "inventions" of the 1940s:
○ Raisin Bran cereal
○ polyester clothing
○ Tupperware
○ Silly Putty
○ the telephone answering machine

New "inventions" of the 1950s:
○ TV dinners and Kentucky Fried Chicken
○ Comet, Pampers, and non-stick cookware
○ UNIVAC, the first electronic digital computer
○ the first computer microchip
○ the credit card

Women were demanding equal rights in the 1950s. In 1956, the Canadian government passed a law that would allow equal pay for equal work, at least in federal government departments and agencies. It would take many more years before this policy spread to private business and industry. (Even today, however, women do not always receive equal pay for equal work.)

In September 1954, sixteen-year-old Marilyn Bell swam across Lake Ontario. She was the first to complete the fifty-two-kilometer swim. Marilyn proved to many people that a woman athlete could endure tough competition without any ill

Marilyn Bell became a hero to all of Canada after she was the first person to swim across Lake Ontario in 1954.

effects to her health. She went on to swim the English Channel in 1955 and the Strait of Juan de Fuca in 1956.

There was little support for amateur sport in the 1950s, but figure skating became very popular in North America. Barbara Ann Scott had captured the hearts of Canadians in the late 1940s. She was the first Canadian to win the world figure skating championship in 1947 and won a gold medal in 1948 at the Olympics. The mayor of Ottawa gave her a car, but she had to give it back when there was a big furor because of her loss of "amateur" standing. Many newborn girls were named "Barbara" during the late 1940s and early 1950s. And every little girl in Canada wanted a Barbara Ann Scott doll for her birthday.

Women in sports still had a long way to go, however. Instead of praising Barbara Ann for her outstanding athletic ability, people talked about her good looks. She was called Canada's "Sweetheart." The same thing happened twenty years earlier, when Ethel Catherwood was called the "Saskatoon Lily" at the 1928 Olympics. The road toward equality for women in sports was an especially long and tough one.

Other popular women athletes of the 1950s:

o Lucile Wheeler, the first Canadian to win a race in world ski competition in 1958

o Anne Heggtveit, Canada's first Olympic skiing gold medallist in the slalom in 1960

Opposite page: Barbara Ann Scott in 1948.

Bobbie, Canada's Female Athlete of the Half-Century, with Lionel Conacher, at left, the Male Athlete of the Half-Century. At right is a representative of the Canadian Press, who awarded the honors. Lionel received a fishing set, and Bobbie received a purse and a $50 bond.

23

Bobbie at Mid-Century

At the end of 1950, Bobbie was selected by sportswriters and broadcasters all across Canada as the "Female Athlete of the Half-Century." Barbara Ann Scott, the "sweetheart" of Canada, came a close second. Bobbie didn't mind. She had always praised Barbara Ann in her column. Bobbie was thrilled that she had been chosen. Her co-workers, her fans, her friends and family were very proud of her. Telegrams, telephone calls,

The male athlete of the half-century was Lionel Conacher. He was nicknamed the "Big Train" for good reason. He had dominated sports in the 1920s and 1930s – football, hockey, baseball, lacrosse, rowing, and boxing. He died of a heart attack at the young age of 53, in the middle of a softball game in 1954.

Above: *The Toronto Hockey League presented Bobbie with a bouquet of red roses, a silver tray and ten pounds of candy upon her nomination as Female Athlete of the Half-Century.* **Bottom:** *Bobbie looking at an earlier photo of herself.*

The members of the gold-medal-winning 400-meter relay team were inducted into Canada's Sports Hall of Fame in 1955. Left to right: Bobbie, Ethel Smith, Florence (Jane) Bell, and Myrtle Cook (with Bobby Kerr, another former Olympic champion).

Also inducted into the new Sports Hall of Fame in 1955:
○ Barbara Ann Scott, world-class figure skater
○ James Naismith, inventor of basketball in 1892
○ Percy Page, coach of the Edmonton Grads women's basketball team
○ Captain Angus Walters, skipper of the famous "Bluenose" schooner
○ Louis Cyr, strong man of the 1800s
○ Percy Williams, winner of the 100 and 200-meter races at the 1928 Olympics

and letters flooded into the *Globe and Mail* offices. Even Foster Hewitt of "Hockey Night in Canada" fame interviewed her. Bobbie was happy that people continued to acknowledge what she had accomplished. She said, "It is nice to know that my small contribution to Canada's athletic life is still remembered, despite the fact that my active days in sport have long been tucked in mothballs."

Along with the other women of the Matchless Six, Bobbie was inducted into Canada's Sports Hall of Fame in 1955. The Hall of Fame had just been established on the CNE grounds in Toronto at a cost of 400,000 dollars. Everyone was excited about having a place where Canada's greatest sports heroes would be honored.

Meanwhile the world around Bobbie was rapidly changing. When Bobbie's family had moved to Toronto in the 1920s, four out of five people were of British stock. By 1960, this was true of only five out of ten people. In 1948, Canada admitted more than 180,000 post-war immigrants, including 65,000 displaced persons. Among those refugees were eight thousand Jews.

In 1951, Bobbie moved away from the family home on Markham Street. Her ~~parents~~ *father* had died and her sisters had

Because of further changes to immigration laws in 1962, thousands of refugees from all over the world were allowed to come to Canada. Many of them came to Toronto. With their different languages, customs and religions, they changed the city.

married. For a time, she shared an apartment with another woman in Toronto's east end. For a year or two, she lived with her sister Ethel, and Ethel's family. Bobbie adored Ethel's children, though she was never prepared to have a family of her own. Bobbie was never one to live a typical woman's life.

Bobbie continued to work at the *Globe and Mail* throughout the 1950s. By 1957, after writing a daily column for twenty years, she became the manager of the public relations department, a less pressured job. For the next eight years, she worked on ways to promote the *Globe and Mail* as Canada's best national newspaper.

After the lull in women's participation in sports in the 1950s, women athletes started to make up for lost time. During the 1960s, they participated in such varied sports as skating, skiing, diving, track, golf, tennis, badminton, table tennis, swimming, and volleyball. Bobbie's favorite team sports were flourishing again in the 1960s – basketball, ice hockey, and softball. Unfortunately, the media mostly ignored them. By then, there was no longer a column such as "Sports Reel" to give the women athletes the attention they deserved

Bobbie retired from the *Globe and Mail* in 1966. It was something she wasn't happy about, but her continuing health problems told her it was time to retire "early." She said she was looking for a part-time job, "so I won't sit back and get lost." She wasn't particular about the kind of work, as long as it didn't involve typing addresses onto envelopes!

After Bobbie left the *Globe and Mail*, there was no other woman sportswriter at the newspaper until 1973, when Christie Blatchford was hired to write mostly about men's professional sports. Bobbie was appalled by the attitudes of male journalists toward women athletes in the 1960s and 1970s. Sportswriters of the time tended to emphasize women athletes as fashion models and sex objects. Of course, journalists had done so before, even in the 1920s. But there was a new crassness in their writing that made Bobbie shudder. Women were not treated with respect. Instead they were applauded or criticized for how they looked.

As late as 1996, a reader wrote a letter to the *Globe and Mail*: "I was extremely disappointed in the *Globe's* almost complete disregard for the world of women's sports."

In 1974, the *Globe and Mail* hired two other women journalists to write about sports. Neither had written about sports before – nor had they been athletes themselves. They weren't very concerned about (or sensitive to) how women athletes were portrayed in newspapers and magazines. They were also totally unaware of the pioneering feminist work done by Bobbie, Myrtle Cook and Alexandrine Gibb – in both athletics and journalism – decades before.

On the stamp: *Canada* · *Fanny Rosenfeld 1928* · *100 m and 400-m relay / 100 m et 400 m relais* · *45*

Bobbie's stamp, issued by Canada Post in 1996.

24
The Legacy of Bobbie Rosenfeld

Late in the evening of November 13, 1969, Bobbie died in her sleep. She was sixty-five years old and had lived a productive, unconventional life for a woman of her time. Funeral services were held at Park Memorial Chapel on Spadina Avenue, not far from the old house on Markham Street where Bobbie had lived with her family for so many years.

Many old friends from her early years of sports, as well as from her days of journalism, came to her funeral. Jane Bell, who attended the funeral, said that when Bobbie died, "a part of myself died, too." Bobbie was buried in the Hebrew Men of England section of Lambton Mills Cemetery, in the west end of the city.

The Bobbie Rosenfeld Award.

After her death, Bobbie received the recognition she deserved. Once every year, people hear of Bobbie Rosenfeld. That's when the plaque named in her honor is given to Canada's Female Athlete of the Year. The winner of the Bobbie Rosenfeld Award is chosen from the results of a poll taken of sports editors and broadcasters across the country. The winner is presented with the award at a formal dinner given by the Sports Federation of Canada.

Some outstanding recipients of the Bobbie Rosenfeld Award:
  Carolyn Waldo (1987–8), synchronized swimming
  Silken Laumann (1991–2), rowing
  Myriam Bédard (1994), biathlon
  Catriona Le May Doan (1998, 2001–2), speed skating
  Perdita Felicien (2003), track

If you travel to Barrie, Ontario, you can see the special bronze plaque that Canada's Historic Sites and Monuments Board placed in Bobbie's honor in 1987. It is fixed to a large stone boulder just outside the Allendale Recreation Centre. Bobbie would be glad to know that children and adults who use the Allendale Centre walk past the plaque on their way to play hockey or baseball or basketball. Sometimes they even stop by the painting of Bobbie that hangs in a prominent spot in the Barrie Sports Hall of Fame at the Centre.

If you are in downtown Toronto, you can stroll through the Bobbie Rosenfeld Park, between the SkyDome and the CN Tower, which the city built in 1991. And in 1996, Canada Post issued five stamps honoring past Olympians, including Bobbie Rosenfeld, Ethel Catherwood, and Percy Williams from the 1928 Olympics.

Bobbie Rosenfeld proved that a girl could play a variety of sports and be spectacular at every one. At the 1928 Olympics, she demonstrated that she could play hard and still play fairly. Later,

In 1981, Bobbie was one of two Canadians inducted into the International Jewish Sports Hall of Fame in Netanya, Israel. The other Canadian was Louis Rubenstein of Montreal, a world champion figure skater of the late 1800s.

FANNY 'BOBBIE' ROSENFELD
(1903 – 1969)

Shortly after her birth in Russia, Fanny Rosenfeld's family emigrated to Canada, settling in Barrie. An all-round athlete, she excelled in hockey, basketball, tennis and softball. She held several long-standing Canadian track and field records and the world record for the 100 metres. 'Bobbie' led the Canadian women's team to victory at the 1928 Amsterdam Olympics with a gold and silver medal. Arthritis ended her athletic career in 1933, after which she became a prominent Toronto sports columnist. In 1949 she was chosen 'Canada's outstanding female athlete of the half-century.'

Fanny Rosenfeld naquit en Russie, mais sa famille immigra bientôt au Canada et s'installa à Barrie. Elle excella au hockey, au ballon panier, au tennis et à la balle molle. En athlétisme, elle établit des records canadiens et réalisa le meilleur temps mondial pour le 100 mètres. En 1928, aux Olympiades d'Amsterdam, elle mena l'équipe canadienne à la victoire, menant ainsi à la conquête de médailles d'or et d'argent. L'arthrite mit fin à sa carrière en 1933 et elle se consacra à la chronique sportive. En 1949, elle fut choisie 'athlète féminine de la première moitié du siècle.'

BOBBIE ROSENFELD PARK

City of Toronto
Department of
Parks and Recreation

Above: Ethel Berman, Bobbie's sister, and Ethel's granddaughter, Tara, look at the plaque unveiled in Barrie in 1987 to commemorate Bobbie's achievements. It was later mounted onto a large boulder. The plaque states that Bobbie was named female athlete of the half-century in 1949, due to confusion over when the half-century ended. She formally received the honor in December 1950.
Bottom: Bobbie Rosenfeld Park, in Toronto.

she showed that even when she couldn't compete anymore, she could still take her love of sports and use it in a positive way. As a strong advocate for women's sports, Bobbie helped make it possible for young women to actively participate today.

Bobbie lived to see the women's 800-meter race come back to the Summer Olympics in 1960. She also saw women's volleyball introduced at the Olympics in 1964, along with the pentathlon and 400-meter race. Had she lived longer, she would have been thrilled to know that women represented almost 40 percent of the total athletes at the 2000 Olympic Games in Sydney, Australia. If Bobbie had lived into our own time, she would have cheered for Hayley Wickenheiser at the 2002 Winter Olympics, when Hayley helped Canada win gold in ice hockey.

In 1999, Nancy Greene (Raine) was named Canada's Athlete of the Century. (Nancy had won gold in the giant slalom and silver in the slalom at the 1968 Olympics in Grenoble and ten races in a row to defend her World Cup title.) Bobbie came sixth in the vote. All the other athletes in the top ten were known for just one sport. Bobbie was the only "complete" athlete.

Most of all, Bobbie would have been proud of the 1994 Amendment to the Olympic Charter: "The IOC strongly encourages ... the promotion of women in sport at all levels and in all structures ... with a view to the strict application of the principle of equality of men and women." Having set the example in the 1928 Olympics, ~~she herself~~ left a lasting legacy.

Bobbie Rosenfeld

The Legacy of Bobbie Rosenfeld

Timeline

1904(?) Born Fanny Rosenfeld in Katrinaslov, Russia, on December 28.

1905 Rosenfeld family leaves Russia and settles in Barrie, Ontario.

1921 Bobbie wins her first trophy at the Great War Veterans Association Track Meet.

1922 Rosenfelds move to Toronto where Bobbie attends Harbord Collegiate and stars on the track and field team.

1923 Bobbie defeats Helen Filkey, the world record holder in the 100-meter race, at the Canadian National Exhibition.

1924 Bobbie wins the Toronto Ladies Grass Courts tennis singles championship.

1925 Bobbie wins five gold and two silver medals at the Ontario Ladies Track and Field Championships.

1927 Bobbie's relay team wins gold in the 440-yard relay at the Millrose Games in New York.

1928 At the Olympic trials in Halifax, Bobbie sets Canadian records that last until 1950 in running broad jump, standing broad jump, and discus.

1928 Bobbie leads her 4 x 100 relay team to a gold, and wins a silver medal in the 100-meter race at the Olympics in Amsterdam; comes fifth in the 800-meter race.

1929 Bobbie defeats Betty Robinson in the 4 x 100 relay race at Millrose Games in New York. Bobbie's team came in second, but Bobbie defeated Betty in her lap of the race.

1929 Bobbie gets a severe case of arthritis.

1931 Bobbie returns to hockey and softball. She is voted the outstanding woman hockey player in Ontario and leads the Ontario softball league in home runs.

1932 Bobbie gets a job writing about sports for the *Montreal Herald*.

1933 At age 29, Bobbie retires from sports forever, after a second attack of arthritis.

1934   Bobbie coaches women's track and field team at British Empire Games in London.

1937   Bobbie begins writing "Sports Reel" for the Toronto *Globe and Mail*.

1946   Bobbie is named Canada's outstanding female athlete in the Canadian Press polls. She receives the same honor in 1947 and 1948.

1947   Bobbie receives the Lou E. Marsh trophy as the outstanding athlete in Canada. She wins it again in 1948.

1948   Bobbie receives the Police Gazette's Gold Cup as the world's outstanding woman athlete.

1950   Bobbie is selected as Canada's "Female Athlete of the Half-Century."

1951   Bobbie receives a Commemoration Scroll from the Canadian Jewish Congress for her extensive contribution to sports.

1955   Along with other members of the Matchless Six, Bobbie is inducted into Canada's Sports Hall of Fame.

1957   Bobbie retires as columnist, and becomes *Globe and Mail* Public Relations Manager.

1966   Bobbie retires from the *Globe and Mail* due to illness.

1969   Bobbie Rosenfeld dies in Toronto on November 13, at the age of 65.

1978   Canadian Press establishes the Bobbie Rosenfeld Award for Canada's Female Athlete of the Year.

1981   Bobbie is inducted into the International Jewish Sports Hall of Fame in Israel, the first Canadian woman athlete to be so honored.

1985   Bobbie becomes one of the first athletes to be named in the Barrie Sports Hall of Fame.

1987   Historic Sites and Monument Board names Bobbie, along with Ned Hanlan, Tom Longboat, and Lionel Conacher, as one of the most important figures in Canadian history.

1991   City of Toronto establishes the Bobbie Rosenfeld Park between the SkyDome and the CN Tower.

1996   Canada Post Corporation issues five stamps honoring past Canadian Olympians. They include Bobbie Rosenfeld, Ethel Catherwood, and Percy Williams.

Adapted from Jewish Women's Archive Website: "JWA – Bobbie Rosenfeld – Timeline." www.jwa.org/exhibits/wov/rosenfeld/tmline.html

Further Reading

About Sports

[no author] *Grace & Glory: A Century of Women in the Olympics*. Washington, D.C.: Multi-Media Partners Ltd., 1996.

Cochrane, Jean, Abby Hoffman, Pat Kincaid. *Women in Canadian Sports*. Toronto: Fitzhenry & Whiteside, 1977.

Kristy, Davida. *Coubertin's Olympics: How the Games Began*. Minneapolis: Lerner Publications Company, 1995.

About Bobbie Rosenfeld

Bryant, Jill. *Amazing Women Athletes*. Toronto: Second Story Press, 2001.

Hehner, Barbara. *The Penguin Book of Canadian Biography for Young Readers*. Volume II. Toronto: Penguin Books, 2002.

About History

Mackay, Claire. *The Toronto Story*. Toronto: Annick Press, 2002. (rev. ed.)

OTHER RESOURCES

On video

"The Matchless Six." Written and produced by Brenda Hennig; directed by Janice Brown. Great North Productions, 1996.

"Bobbie Rosenfeld: The Natural Athlete." Written and directed by Martin Harbury, with Carrie Madu as line producer. Canadians 3 Alberta Productions, 1999. Program first telecast on January 26, 2000.

On the Internet

Amateur Athletic Foundation of Los Angeles: www.aafla.org

CBC: Foster Hewitt interviews Bobbie Rosenfeld (28 Dec. 1950), and Norm Perry interviews Bobbie Rosenfeld (15 July 1964): archives.cbc.ca.

Canadian Association for the Advancement of Women and Sport and Physical Activity: www.caaws.ca

International Olympic Committee: www.olympic.org

Jewish Women's Archive Exhibit: www.jwa.org/exhibits/rosenfeld/

Acknowledgements

My personal thanks and appreciation go to:

Bruce Beacock, Archivist, Simcoe County Archives, Minesing, Ontario

Karen Czaniecki, Administrator, Heritage Toronto

David Hart, Archivist, Holy Blossom Temple, Toronto

Julie Kirsh, Director of Electronic Information, the *Toronto Sun*, Toronto

Ellen Millar, Assistant Archivist, Simcoe County Archives, Minesing, Ontario

Janice Rosen, Director, Canadian Jewish Congress National Archives, Montreal

Prof. Danny Rosenberg, Chair, Department of Physical Education and Kinesiology, Brock University, St. Catharines, Ontario

Jennifer Sartori, Jewish Women's Archive

Ellen Scheinberg, Director, Ontario Jewish Archives, Toronto

Howard Schmertz, Meet Director Emeritus, Verizon Millrose Games, New York

Allan Stewart, Executive Director, Canada's Sports Hall of Fame, Toronto

Librarians at: Toronto Reference Library (especially in the Baldwin room and *Toronto Star* newspaper room), Barrie Public Library, City of Toronto Archives

At Second Story Press: Margie Wolfe, for having faith in me; Laura McCurdy, for pulling the innumerable threads together; editor Sarah Silberstein Swartz, for her bright intellect and firm hand.

Meryl Arbing, Robert Bennett, Ethel Berman, Ruth Chellin, Jack Cooper, Robert Fulford, Judith Ghert, Carmen Horvath, Emil Horvath, Bushie Kamin, Bernard Katz, Leonard Levy, Bob Loft, Judy Nisenholt, Rivanne Sandler, Tom Sankey, Judy Saul, Sydell Waxman

I would also like to acknowledge the sources for quotations used in this book:

Chapter 6, p. 31: Constance Hennessy, quoted in Douglas Fisher and S.F. Wise, *Canada's Sporting Heroes* (Toronto: General Publishing Company, 1974), 79.

Chapter 8, p. 34: Pierre de Coubertin, quoted in "The Matchless Six" by Ron Hotchkiss, *The Beaver* (October-November, 1993), 23.

Chapter 10, p. 42: Lou E. Marsh, from "Canada's Olympic Team Chuck Full of Confidence," *Toronto Daily Star* (11 July 1928), 10.

Chapter 10, p. 44: Alexandrine Gibb, from "Banner of Victory for Canadian Girls," *Toronto Daily Star* (12 July 1928), 12.

Chapter 13, p. 55: Alexandrine Gibb, from "Canada at the Olympics," *Maclean's* (1 October 1928), 46.

Chapter 13, p. 56: Bobbie Rosenfeld, from "Girls are in Sports for Good," *Chatelaine* (July 1933), 5.

Chapter 14, p. 59: Jane Bell, quoted in "The Matchless Six" by Ron Hotchkiss, *The Beaver* (October-November 1993), 37.

Chapter 18, p. 75: Foster Hewitt, from the *Toronto Daily Star* (25 November 1930), 25.

Chapter 21, p. 82: Bobbie Rosenfeld, from "Girls are in Sports for Good," *Chatelaine,* (July 1933), 29.

Bibliography

BOOKS ABOUT SPORTS

Blue, Adrianne. *Faster, Higher, Further: Women's Triumphs and Disasters at the Olympics.* London: Virago Press Limited, 1988.

Cosentino, Frank and Glynn Leyshon. *Olympic Gold: Canada's Winners in the Summer Games.* Toronto: Holt, Rhinehart and Winston, 1975.

Guttmann, Allen. *The Olympics: A History of the Modern Games.* Chicago: University of Illinois Press, 2002. (2ND ed.)

Hall, M. Ann. *The Girl and the Game: A History of Women's Sport in Canada.* Peterborough, ON: Broadview Press, 2002.

Kidd, Bruce. *The Struggle for Canadian Sport.* Toronto: University of Toronto Press, 1996.

Morrow, Don et al. *A Concise History of Sport in Canada.* Toronto: Oxford University Press, 1989.

Smith, Lissa. *Nike is a Goddess: The History of Women in Sports.* New York: Atlantic Monthly Press, 1999.

BOOKS ABOUT HISTORY

[no author] *National Geographic: Eyewitness to the 20TH Century.* Washington, D.C.: National Geographic Society, 1998.

Abbott, Elizabeth (ed.) *Chronicle of Canada.* Montreal: Chronicle Publications, 1990.

Abella, Irving and Harold Troper. *None Is Too Many: Canada and the Jews of Europe* 1933-1948. Toronto: Lester Orpen Dennys, 1982.

Bothwell, Robert. *Our Century: The Canadian Journey in the Twentieth Century.* Toronto: McArthur, 2000.

Brownstone, David M. *Timelines of the* 20TH *Century.* Boston: Little, Brown, 1996.

Gillmor, Don. *Canada: A People's History.* Toronto: McClelland and Stewart, 2000.

Speisman, Stephen. *The Jews of Toronto: A History to* 1937. Toronto: McClelland & Stewart, 1979.

Tulchinsky, Gerald. *Taking Root: The Origins of the Canadian Jewish Community.* Toronto: Lester Publishing Limited, 1992.

BOOKS ABOUT BOBBIE ROSENFELD

Watson, Patrick. *The Canadians: Biographies of a Nation.* Toronto: McArthur & Company, 2000.

Photo Credits

Front Cover: All photos at left from Canada's Sports Hall of Fame, photo at right from Sun Media Corp.

Back Cover: Canada's Sports Hall of Fame

Title page: Sun Media Corp.

Page XII: Canada's Sports Hall of Fame

Pages 1 and 3: Pringle and Booth / NATIONAL ARCHIVES OF CANADA / C-047042

Page 6: Collier Street in Barrie, from a postcard. 969-83. E6 B6 R6B S6 Sh3. Courtesy of Simcoe County Archives

Page 8: City of Toronto Archives, Fonds 1244 Item 9175

Page 12: City of Toronto Archives, Fonds 1244 Item 474

Pages 15 and 24: Sun Media Corp.

Page 16: Barrie Collegiate Institute, B6 R3B S3 Sh1. Courtesy of Simcoe Country Archives

Page 20: Courtesy of Toronto Public Library (TRL): T 13988

Page 21 (top): Jewish Butcher Shop, Toronto, June 1923. M.O. Hammond (Archives of Ontario, F 1075, #649. I0001138)

Page 21 (bottom): John Boyd / NATIONAL ARCHIVES OF CANADA / PA-084812

Page 22 (left): City of Toronto Archives, Series 372, Subseries 11, Item 94

Page 22 (right): City of Toronto Archives, Fonds 1231 Item 2173

Page 26: Courtesy of Toronto Public Library (TRL): T 10032

Page 28: NATIONAL ARCHIVES OF CANADA / C-147600 and C-147602

Page 30: John Boyd / NATIONAL ARCHIVES OF CANADA / PA-061175

Page 32: Canada's Sports Hall of Fame

Page 34: Canada's Sports Hall of Fame

Page 35: Canada's Sports Hall of Fame

Page 37: Toronto Port Authority

Page 40: Canada's Sports Hall of Fame

Page 41: Sun Media Corp.

Page 42: *Toronto Star*

Page 43: Canada's Sports Hall of Fame

Page 44: Reprinted with permission from *The Globe and Mail*

Page 47: Sun Media Corp.

Page 49: City of Toronto Archives, Fonds 1244 Item 8172

Page 53: *Toronto Star*

Page 57: City of Toronto Archives, Fonds 1266 Item 14109

Page 60: Courtesy of Meryl Arbing

Pages 64 and 67 (bottom): NATIONAL ARCHIVES OF CANADA / PA-150998

Page 67 (top): NATIONAL ARCHIVES OF CANADA / PA-151007

Page 70: NATIONAL ARCHIVES OF CANADA / PA-151008

Page 74: Canada's Sports Hall of Fame

Page 77: NATIONAL ARCHIVES OF CANADA / PA-151004

Page 79: NATIONAL ARCHIVES OF CANADA / PA-151001

Page 81: City of Toronto Archives, Fonds 1266 Item 14632

Page 85: Bobbie with gift car. E13 B3 R4B S3 Sh3, Bk. 35 p/156. Courtesy of Simcoe County Archives

Page 80: Sun Media Corp.

Page 86: Sun Media Corp.

Page 88: Reprinted with permission from *The Globe and Mail*

Page 89: *Toronto Star*

Page 90: Courtesy of the *Barrie Examiner*

Page 94: Canada, Dept. of the Interior / NATIONAL ARCHIVES OF CANADA / C-026742

Page 95: NATIONAL ARCHIVES OF CANADA / PA-168131

Page 98: Canadian Jewish Congress National Archives

Page 101: City of Toronto Archives, Fonds 1266 Item 25807

Page 104: City of Toronto Archives,

Fonds 1266 Item 25379

Page 106: Sun Media Corp.

Page 107: Photo by Meryl Arbing

Page 108: Sun Media Corp.

Pages 112, 113 and 115: Reprinted with permission from *The Globe and Mail*

Page 117: NATIONAL ARCHIVES OF CANADA / e000761740

Page 121: Canada's Sports Hall of Fame

Page 123: Frank Royal / NATIONAL ARCHIVES OF CANADA / PA-112373

Page 124: Canada's Sports Hall of Fame

Page 125, both photographs: Canada's Sports Hall of Fame

Page 126: Sun Media Corp.

Page 130: Courtesy of Canada Post

Page 131: Ontario Jewish Archives, plaque given to Bobbie Rosenfeld by the Canadian Press, 1950, artifact #311, Box 19

Page 132: Ontario Jewish Archives, medallion given to Bobbie by the International Jewish Sports Hall of Fame in 1981, artifact #330, Box 19

Page 133 (top): Photo by Erik Christensen, reprinted with permission from *The Globe and Mail*

Page 133 (bottom): Photo by Meryl Arbing

Page 148: Photo by Meryl Arbing

Index

About the Author

Anne Dublin is a teacher-librarian in Toronto. Like Bobbie Rosenfeld, Anne came to Canada at a very young age. She has previously written short stories, articles, poetry, and a novel called *Written on the Wind*.